Here in suburbia, residents complain that they don't have as many Coach bags or German luxury cars as their peers. Their children have to suffer three meals a day with healthy food, but don't have the latest devices. Complaints about square footage, brands and material things (or the lack thereof) are often heard at PTA meetings and soccer fields. But what if these suburban residents' very lives were in danger? What if they suffered hunger, abuse and the constant uncertainty of poverty or underemployment?

Fewer than five miles away, their neighbors aren't concerned with granite countertops so much as having a roof of any type over their heads. They're not concerned with whether their children can compete in the electronic gadget wars, but whether they can actually feed them. Their parents lived the same way. Their mothers died at the hands of domestic abuse. As children, they were physically and sexually abused and neglected. School was not a priority. Violence, drugs, and prostitution were always just a breath away. Having survived childhood without the guidance to become adults, how are they living as adults?

To think that in the richest country on earth, people live without hope, separated from the American dream, is unconscionable. It is something that many middle class Americans either sweep under the rug, or truly have no knowledge of, due to a lack of exposure to this reality. To change this culture is going to take understanding, compassion and creativity. But, before understanding can change the situation, light must shine on the severity and pervasive nature of poverty in neighborhoods not far from our own.

I am white. I grew up in middle class America. Few of my classmates were anything but white children of middle class Americans. We had financial struggles from time to time. I wasn't always dressed as stylishly as my peers. But, I never worried as a child about where my next meal would come from.

After feeling very poor at my expensive Midwestern college, I graduated into a stark real world. There, I quickly learned that my background was no preparation for the reality which is daily life for too many Americans.

I was young and idealistic. I thought the problems of poverty could be overcome with mere effort. So, I enrolled as a VISTA (Volunteer in Service to America), described as the domestic Peace Corps. I was to serve in Springfield, Ohio, my college town. Having graduated with an English major, I was excited to be working in the area of adult literacy.

I was truly shocked that first year out of college. As every tutor did, I enrolled in the Tutor Training Program, hosted by my organization at the Warder Literacy Center in Springfield. I had never met any adult who couldn't read. It was something I had given little thought to as I routinely read 1000 pages a week in college. But, in 1992, the statistics showed that one in five adults was functionally illiterate.

On my tiny stipend from the government (I think it was about $700 per month), I found myself unable to pay bills with my real income. Rent, utilities, food and basic needs were not attainable at that level. However, I did have a health plan, not that I used it at age 22.

I don't remember many specific stories from that year. But, I do remember the fundamental shift it caused in my psyche. It became a window to the perspective that would come later. I couldn't live among struggle and futility and not be affected. The year was more than a financial hardship for me. It would put me in debt for many years. But, unlike the people with whom I worked, I had alternate means. I could get and manage credit. I also had the safety net of a middle class family, if I had ever truly needed to fall into it.

Fast forward a year and I've moved to live near my paternal grandmother. She had retired from the New York State Commission on Quality of Care, after serving as a Psychiatric Nurse on the forefront of rehabilitative treatment innovation. She was responsible for opening a store in a psychiatric center, staffed by patients, and a halfway house (now called a community residence) in the 70s.

With her connections, I was able to get an interview in psychiatric outpatient treatment. Working with outpatients who were involved with educational or vocational treatment, I was opened to a whole new wealth of experience.

Of course, I had worked with adult literacy students who had psychiatric disabilities, but not as a specific part of treatment, and not necessarily on an intense individual basis. So, when I started my new job, I went to the library and checked out a stack of books on everything from major mental illnesses to personality disorders. I did this before I even had furniture.

Living downtown at the time, I recall falling asleep on my living room floor, having diagnosed myself with several mental illnesses after a night of reading. I awoke to the very unsettling vision of a man standing in my window directly above me, by virtue of the small roof over the basement apartment at the level of my living room window. It was a slow recognition on my part, followed by terror. I was green in every way. Life on my own, psychiatric outpatient treatment, and the entire world outside of my previous experience was opening before me in ways I hadn't expected.

With my head full of research, I went to work in a supported employment setting in the affirmative business model, working side by side with outpatient mental health consumers who were learning skills, earning full wages and managing their symptoms through vocational treatment.

It was during this time that I met a woman, whose history I didn't know. She was enjoying making soup, as I recall. I wanted to open a dialog with her, so I asked her where she learned to cook. I imagine that she was a little skeptical of me. So, I asked her if she learned from her mother. This was my first introduction to just how inexperienced I was. She had never really lived with her mother. She had been in foster care and group housing...and I had reminded her of it.

It didn't take long to develop some wisdom and insight into possibly troublesome topics. When you're working in human services, it is critical to mature into someone who can be rarely shocked, otherwise it's almost as if your lack of experience can be immediately sensed, thereby making your good intentions all but imperceptible.

After two and a half years of very low wages and several additional part-time jobs to make ends meet, I left human services to work with a friend in construction management and subsequently in playground design. By this time, four years later, I had finally achieved a living wage and some measure of financial stability. But, something was missing. Not being able to positively affect the lives of others was making work seem solely self-serving. So I began to seek a position in human services once again.

This time, I entered the realm of adult education in the State University of New York system and moved to a private, not for profit a year later, to accept a teaching and training role working with recipients of aid from State and Federal programs. The program was designed to bring computer literacy and job skills to individuals who were unemployed or underemployed. Through the years, the funding came from a variety of sources including the New York State Department of Social Services, Department of Labor and from the Federal Housing Authority.

During eight weeks of intense training in computer skills, soft skills and resume and portfolio development, students would take their skills in Microsoft Word, Excel, PowerPoint and Explorer to either obtain or upgrade their employment. If they were successful in landing a job within 30 days of course completion and held it for at least 90 days, they earned a refurbished computer with the Microsoft Suite so that they could continue to "bridge the digital divide" as we used to say.

Students in this program wrangled with a host of employment barriers ranging from disabilities, low educational levels, drug addiction, domestic violence issues, homelessness, single parenting responsibilities, lack of transportation, and criminal histories, just to name a few. Part of my job was to troubleshoot solutions to these barriers and plan for contingencies so that they could not only obtain employment, but also remain at work successfully.

On a daily basis, there were obstacles to survival, such as non-supportive spouses or family members hunting and threatening students, evictions, a lack of food to feed the family, no appropriate childcare and many others, often occurring all at once. I began to see that "pulling themselves up by the bootstraps" may not be so easy, because many of my students didn't even have boots –literally.

Class after class, there were hundreds of students who came into my office during the course of their studies and told me their stories, often through tears and utter despair. These were people who wanted to work, who wanted a piece of the American pie. But for many reasons, they had trouble getting a fork to eat that pie. After hearing some of their stories, I was amazed that some of them were alive, much less able to get work.

Following, are true stories as told to me by women I've known for over ten years.

Sonia
Where it started

I was told [I was born] July 21, 1967, but that's just, they switched it from my natural, my real date of birth, because I was kidnapped from my mom when I was three. So, I've always celebrated the day I was told even though I know that's not actually it.

I've never had a birth certificate. I've seen one once when I was a little girl. This was when they took me out of hiding. I was …I was hidden from 3 to 6 and 1/2 after my mom, I guess after she died and they buried her I was taken out of hiding. That's when I was given away. I guess too, this was his (my dad's) parents, his mother and his grandmother. They gave me to them.

When I was first taken, there were a lot of trees. It was summer. The sun was shining nice and bright. But, at the same time, it was gloomy, gloomy trees… I think my mom lived somewhere deep in the woods, because I can remember steep hills…there were a lot of trees.

I just know what they told me her name was. My earliest memory of her is the only memory of her I have and that's when he showed up in the red truck. I could tell she didn't trust him because she kept saying, "Bring my baby back. Bring her back. He was like, "I'm gonna take her to the store to get some ice cream." And that was it.

I can remember we got on this highway…I was looking at the sides and it was the first time I was ever on a highway. It was like the white concrete on the sides. I forget which state you go through on the highway, but it's exactly like I remember when I was a little girl and he took me.

Now, I know it was somewhere in Jersey. She's not from there, wasn't born there, but she was living there at the time. It's funny 'cause I was told my name was Tonya Morgan. My mother's last name was Morgan, but he's a Graham. My dad, so called dad, he's a Graham.

They didn't live in the same house. I can remember him showing up. I have different dreams where I'm sitting on a step and all I can hear is screaming...there's a dim light by the door and I can't get in because the door is locked. All I can hear is crying and yelling and screaming and the then all the sudden I wake up. That was a part of some memory. I know someone behind there was hurtin' my mom.

Now as I look back, and what I know of him now, he was a womanizer, player. He went through women like he changed his pants. Given the way I remember her last words to be, she didn't trust him. She probably didn't want him anymore. The way I figured, to get back at her he would come by and get me and never took me back to hurt her, because through the years, he didn't want me. He didn't never take care of me. But he was around always for negative things.

It was something he did to get back at her, because even with their family, even when I was little, even when I said I'd seen my birth certificate, I tried to read it and it was snatched out of my hand and he ripped it up. I thought it was odd at the time. I'm like "won't I need that later on in life?" "No, no you don't need to see that. It's none of your business." It was my birth certificate. How was it not my business? I was a little girl then. And you know when adults are like, "I know what I'm talking about."

My dad's family – they was from the South and they was... I say mean. His mom, I never really did know her. She was never there and when she did come around, all she did when she was in the house for two or three days was ...I was always getting beat at, cussed at.

Whenever I stayed with him was whatever woman's house from [ages] three to six. And then there was an accident where I was in a pool of my own blood. He took me from there and hid me at this other woman's house.

I'll never forget it. I'll never forget that. I stood in a puddle, literally puddle of my own blood. It was a little small puddle. I had these little white sneakers, like the tennis sneakers. And I'm laughing 'cause the outfit I had on was very colorful. They were the only clothes I had at the time. I can remember. It was yellow capris, with black and white. Then, I had on this shirt. It was striped it had so many colors on it.

At the time, you know how little kids is. I remember the woman. I'll never forget her name: Melissa. And he left out to go to work. He had just took me from my mom, so I was like three or four – in between. Her kitchen and my bedroom was the same, 'cause I had a little cot in the corner. It's so weird 'cause she was sitting and I came into the living room, where she was sitting to watch TV. I sat in front and I looked back at her cause I didn't want to be there. In my mind I had said "I'm just going to look through the stuff."

You know how kids are. She's like, "Leave it alone." I did it deliberately. I remember. I just kept looking through it. So, she's like, "Go sit on your bed." I went and sat on the bed and I had all these toys. When my dad had brought them in like the night before, I can remember him saying. "These are toys I got from your mom." So that was the only thing I had to remember her and I remember I had one of those old telephones. You know like kids play with. And I was pretending like I was talking to my mom. I was telling her everything that was going on.

At the same time, I could see this shadow cause her walls was painted white. Her house was clean. The house was clean. I was watching the shadow of the TV on the wall and she came in and, "ooh you watching tv? I told you!" She snatched the phone out of my hand and started beating me with it. I screamed. I stood there and looked down and as the blood was gooshing, she started panicking. She was trying to stop the blood. She said, "Stand there." And as I stood there she ran in the bathroom to get a rag. That's when I ran out the door and it was an apartment. I'm thinking we was on the top floor because, I was small and it seemed like such a long way down. It seemed dark. And it was creepy. The hallway was dark and creepy. I almost made it to the door and as I got there, to the door to go outside this old person picked me up and I guess they knew her, and brought me back to the apartment. I was like, "No, no, no! I wanna get out." "No, we're gonna take you back." So, the old guy took me back again. Today, I think it was a friend of my dad's.

When I got home – she was like, "I'm gonna tell your dad what you did." And I was like, "No, I'm gonna tell him what YOU did. And he's gonna get you, cause look what you did. You bust my head!" When he came home… she stopped the blood. I laid down and when he came in, I was like, "Look what she did." And his words to me were, "Maybe you deserved it."

Sonia
After he took me

He stayed there for a few years [with Melissa]. I never left the house.
After that is was good for a little minute and my dad was a person who
had a temper. Whatever was around him, and he always cooked, he'd
just grab and hit me with it. The day that he hit me with a butcher knife,
he was in the kitchen cooking and I wanted something and he was like,
"No." I think it was his attention I wanted. He was like, "Get away from
me." I was like, "No!" I wanted him to do something and the next thing I
knew he picked it up and I threw my hand up and this thumb right here- I
got hit on the thumb and got cut. He looked at it and ran me in the
kitchen and ran some water on it and wrapped it up and that was that.

I remember when I was first being taught my ABCs, this will tell you how
young I was. I didn't even know my ABC's. It was one evening, late, late
one night and I was supposed to...remember the chalkboards with the
letters on them? I had one of them. I was sitting in the kitchen/bedroom,
on the floor and I was supposed to have been practicing. I was trying.
You know, I was the A, the B, the C. But then I kept hearing the moaning
and the groaning. And I was so small at the time, I remember standing up
and they was in the room and I stood at the door and I thought he was
killing the woman. And I stood there and they looked up and seen me. I
got so scared I ran and sat in my little corner in the kitchen on the little
cot. And he came in. I got my butt tore up that night...so bad. He never
did explain to me what he was doing.

The night after that, this is when I was first raped. I realize it now that's
what it is, but then I thought it was something I had did and it was my
fault. I'm still...if I stood next to this car, I couldn't even see over the car.
That's how little I was. Him and Melissa was goin' out. They had been
drinking. I also was a bed wetter 'cause I was so afraid to get up at night
to go to the bathroom, and if I peed in the bed I'd still get a beating. So,
they was drinking and he gave me the can. This was the first time I had a
drink, too. The can was glistening and we was sittin' at the table and he

was talking about going out. He had the can and I went, "Ooh can I try it?" And he said, "Yeah, maybe it'll stop you from peeing in the bed."

But then, as they were talking about going out they were talking about leaving me with some guy. I was like, "Please, please don't leave me with him. Don't leave me with him." He was like, "He ain't gonna bother you. He better not do nothing to you."

So that night, when they went out, this man came. I couldn't tell you his name, but I remember he smelled, now I know it was beer. It reeked. So, him and Melissa left. And we're sitting down and he got to talking to me. I got to talking and somehow I got to where I started asking him questions, 'cause I was afraid to ask my dad what I had seen that night.

He said, "What happened?" I said, "Well, what is it when a man is moaning and groaning. What is this?" I remember the man saying, "Oh, I'll show you." And I stood up and in the kitchen, I'll never forget it. It was - I was next to a sink in the kitchen. I remember 'cause the paint was yellow. I could barely see over the sink, but my little hands was on the sink. He was behind me. And I remember it being real painful. But this is the weird part -that was kinda confusing, cause at one point it started feeling good. Then he stopped. My dad and them came home and I never said anything about it. And he was like, "That's what your dad and the lady was doing. And that's what two people do when they love each other." Wow, that's...oh snap, that's where I got that thought of sex was love.

After that that's when something happened and they broke up. Then there was the fat woman. Chubby. He was hardly ever around there. Actually, he never was there. He was there. He wasn't there all the time. That was another woman he must have been messing with. I don't remember him being there I whole lot. I remember him coming and going. I hated Chubby cause every day I was being beat. She was the one, she cut my hair real short and she dyed it orange or reddish color. She had two kids. One was a girl and one was a boy. Chubby used to walk around naked all the time. Oh I hated it. She was big and fat and yuck.

Her kids would do stuff and I got beatings for it. At one point, this was the first time I ran away. I remember I was on the boardwalk. I was a little girl. Everyone looked like giants to me. Now I know it was in Atlantic City. Back then I didn't know where, when I was younger...since I lived in Atlantic City, I know that's where it was.

After Chubby, I stayed at Chubby's for a few years. Each time he left me somewhere, it was a different woman. Their kids was always older than me. So, I was either being abused by the woman, if not the woman, it was the kids.

After Chubby, then he met Jane. Now, I kinda liked Jane 'cause as long as she was around she protected me. But when she left in the morning and went to work that's when hell day started, 'cause she had grown kids. She had two girls and two boys. One of the girls wasn't there. The youngest girl, who was still older than me was Julia. Phew... There was times, because I had such a fear of him, to me he was like this giant -this big giant man with a deep voice. I was always fearful of him, always afraid cause of his height and his size and his voice. Julia and them, as I look back, I realize, the way they got me to do things, they used my fear of my dad. Like, "if you don't do so and so, we're gonna tell." And they knew he didn't ask no questions. He didn't talk. Whatever he had in his hand that's what I got beat with. Or if he didn't have anything he'd find it.

So, on any given day I was made to go down on, Julia would hold me, hold me down, while one of her brothers, one named Matt and one named Bart. One would have their penis in my mouth while the other was doing...was having sex. And this went on it could be an hour to two hours. However long and they made a game out of it. They would say different things, and if I got it wrong, whatever the boys wanted to do Julia would hold me down. And they would do it. This went on for years. They was young teenagers. I was the baby.

Even down to birthdays, I remember, I didn't really have a birthday or celebrate or anything. I always went to their birthdays and it was like I was just thrown in there. They'd be getting gifts and everything and I didn't get anything.

The day they took me away from them, we was walking coming from the store and Bart was with me. I pleaded and I pleaded and they didn't believe me. He talked me into going into the bushes. I'll never forget this day, cause I kept saying, "This is wrong. I'm a little girl. You shouldn't be doing this with a little girl. You shouldn't be doing this with me. I'm supposed to be your sister." And he was like, "No, no, no. I'm not your brother. I'm just, you know, trying to make you feel good." He told me... I laid down in the bushes and what happened was, Julia, one of them caught him on top of me. It was on the side of the house. I'll never forget. And my dad and Jane was sitting in the bedroom in the room and came to call, "Come on in here." And Jane said, "I don't like her. She doesn't listen. She's not this, she's not that. I want her out of my house." And I remember standing there saying, "Your son, your son coaxed me. Your son put me down on the ground. Your son held me." "No, no, no he wouldn't a did nothing like that unless you told him. You coaxed him."

After that he took me. The last place he hid me, and I was there until they put my mother in the ground, that was so far deep in the woods, no one would have ever found me. My mother wouldn't have found me. It was almost like the South where there's a house here and 50-100-200 there's another house. My friends was a turtle, a goose. I would just walk and there was trees for miles. There was a road. Every maybe four or five hours you may see a car or a truck.

I was there up until – I didn't have birthdays then, so that's the strangest part, trying to figure out how old I was. I'm not really sure. I know I was young. I was a little girl cause there was never birthdays. There was never celebrations until after he took me out of hiding.

Before he took me from Atlantic City, I had a dream where there was a casket and a white fence and there was people, and in the dream someone is saying, "Your mom is dead. Your mom is dead." When I woke up I asked him, "Where is my mom? Is she dead?" And he was like, "How did you know that?" It was raining that day. We took a walk and he said, "I need to talk to you. Yes, she died. She died a couple of days ago. " He also said he was going to move me somewhere else.

Then I was there so long until one day a bunch of people showed up in a powder blue/baby blue station wagon. There was nothin' but old folks in it. Adults in it. I looked. I was on the road playing and walking and they went in the house. It must have been some of his relatives' or somebody he knew. They didn't have a bathroom, but they was sweet. This may sound strange, but there was a sense of peace because I wasn't being touched. I wasn't being beat. Even though there wasn't no kids or no one else around but just the animals, I was a little happy...even though there wasn't other kids. There was an outhouse and not a bathroom and we had to pee in a bucket.

Then when he took me and gave me to the people who showed up in the car, we got on the highway again. Now I know it was a highway and we was leaving the state. But back then, I didn't know. Then, when we got to Connecticut, I remember thinking, "Finally, I'm with a family. I can be happy." But then it wasn't like that.

Gloria
The Beginning

I was born in Orlando, Florida. From there, when I was a little child about 2 years old, my mother brought us up to New York City and Brooklyn, New York. I got raised in Brooklyn, New York. We lived in apartment down in Park Slope, Sunset Park and up by Prospect Park.

My mother was at home with the children, cuz there was six of us. There were six of us living at home and we would go to school within the area out there. And my father wasn't there. He was...I'm not quite sure - with his sisters or something like that. Him and my mom broke up when I was a little baby and they didn't get along too well and they'd fight a lot and stuff and argue. So, they went on their separate ways and stuff like that. So, he used to come on every weekend and come and see us. He used to bring his potato chips and stuff and we'd be all excited, because potato chips then was like 5 cents. And he used to have my uncle with him and we used to call him "Uncle Bill." Oh no we didn't, we called him, "Daddy Bill."

We was on Social Service. Back then we called it Welfare. We was the Welfare kids. My mother, a certain time of the month, I guess the first and 16th, they used to give us these vouchers and Medicaid cards. They were made out of paper. We had vouchers and we'd go to the projects and there'd be a long line with shopping carts. Back in the days, it was so hard to get food back then. So they gave us these vouchers and we'd go on line and we'd get cheese and eggs and some kind of salmon meat and they used to have these cans with chicken in it and stuff like that. The main thing was the cheese. Everyone used to love that, because we used to do the grilled cheese all the time. But the line was so long downtown in Brooklyn in the projects. You could see everyone standing on line with their shopping carts and going blocks and blocks and blocks.

We had some type of vouchers, or Medicaid, or what, 'cuz the doctors used to come to the house back then. They used to come to the house to see us and everything like that. What happens is we'd be on that line for two or three hours at a time and it be cold. But we'd still be on that line to get food to bring it home. We'd get boxes because there was six of us. And after we'd get it home and everything, she usually make our grilled cheese. My mother'd be home most of the time, 'cuz when we'd go to school in the area, we'd come home and she'd be there.

We didn't get a chance to ride on the school bus. Back then, we had to live a certain amount of miles and we lived a long distance from there. We didn't have tights and long johns and nothing like that. My mother had little bobby socks and stuff, and little dresses. And we'd walk to school and be freezing cold out there. We walked from 19th Street and First Avenue up to 15th or 12th and 6th Avenue 'cause we didn't ride the bus.

It was kind of scary in some ways, because of the fact of, me and my sisters, we used sometimes only have two or three dresses. And we had to wash our own stuff and make sure it was ready for the next day and stuff. It seemed like it was like down south going to school, 'cuz we used to walk these miles and stuff and there was nothing back then to participate in. There was no after school center. It wasn't...the only way you was in after school center was if you was on punishment or you got in trouble and your parents had to come and pick you up. They kept you there in the office.

But it got to a point, I enjoyed school, but then I'd not go. I'd go to the park right there, right next to the school and play in the park. The truant officer would come out. I don't know what was on my mind. We were outside on the swing right next to the school. The park was right here and the school was right here. We wasn't thinkin'. We was young, and we was too scared to go anywhere further from the school. So we was in the park and he'd come outside and bring us back inside. He'd ask, "What's going on?" And it'd be either somebody picking at us, or you know, being bullies to us in school. And that was one of my things there. I didn't have that many clothes and they be dirty and stuff like that. We use to try to wash them the best way we can and people used to tease us and stuff. We kind of got over it a little bit and my mom would bring us back to school.

But there was no after-school center. Or at the time, they did have tutors. But they didn't have enough to really go around, and they didn't really have too many teachers and stuff. But I remember when I was in school, I think I was in 4th or 5th grade, President Kennedy got shot. Everybody was crying and I kept wondering, "Why they crying? What's this guy?" I didn't know who it was. I used to get picked on and there was this guy Milton, a little Spanish guy. He was this short...and he'd tell everyone to stop bothering me or he'd beat them up.

I used to get my work - I couldn't understand a lot of things in class, because we didn't get to the get the chance to read anything. We had our little chores we had to clean up - sweep up, and stuff in the house. We wasn't allowed to sit on the furniture. We had to sit on the floor and my mother always used to tell us, "You can't be in grown folks business." So if she'd get company or something...we always had to sit on the floor with our legs crossed. And you know, disciplining us, if she's see us on the couch she'd come, Bam, knock us out and get right back down there. And we ALWAYS eat at 6:00. Everybody eat together at 6:00 - can't be no talking or anything. You have to eat your food, get ready to go to bed at 8:00. The only thing I think after we got home from school, we could go outside, after we did our homework and stuff like that. We used to play double Dutch. We used to get on the little go carts we made out of crate boxes, put the little legs on it from the baby stroller. We'd take the big wheels off, put it on the front and back and get the crate boxes, I think it was milk crate boxes. They'd be wood and they'd be nailed to the thing. We'd do hopscotch and everything.

We used to have a church right across the street from us. It was a safe neighborhood. But back then, they had the racial thing going on, too. We lived in an Italian neighborhood and we had two buildings of black people. It was 263 and 265. Every now and then we'd get a group of Italian guys coming down the street and want to fight. They'd throw stuff through the windows, break the windows. I said, "I'll open the windows so they don't break it." They threw it and it broke both windows. I was like, "Oh I didn't know that would happen!" We lived on the second floor. They would come by and raid and they'd throw all kinds of stuff. We used to be scared and stuff like that and try to figure out what's going on. We were so small we didn't know. It was just those two buildings down in that area. It's more like Park Slope.

We didn't have any money to get on the bus. We used to jump in the back door and be ducking down and like that. But the bus was only like twenty cents back then. Then if we couldn't do that we'd jump on and hold on to the thing on the back of the bus. These busses were so old. They was round lookin'.   But the neighborhood was a nice, safe neighborhood. I lived on 20th Street, between 5th and 6th and the school was on 18th Street, between 7th and 8th. They also had rebuilt another school for 8th graders because there was so many 8th graders in the area. That was on 18th Street. So all the eighth graders went to that school and the other school was called IS88. They didn't call it Junior High School, they just called it Intermediate School number 88, and it was a nice school. You'd go under it to get into the building. The old school, public school was eighth graders.

This lady lived next door. There was a whole group all down the row, and then this was this bakery. They made cakes, pies, everything. Then there was this other one, around the other corner... made bread you could smell two blocks away. The bread smelled good. And this Italian lady who lived next door, on the first floor she used to tell my mother, "Can your daughter go get me some bread first thing in the morning, like 10:00, and I pay her?" Like that. And she was like, "Surprise. She going to pay you $10. Yeah, you're going to do that." And, plus, give me bread. And still today, I still like Italian bread. So every time about 10:00 my mother sent me over to her house. I'd get the money. I'd go get about 20 loaves of bread and then I would get three extra for myself. When I'd go around there, they'd be just taking it off the pans and it's hot. It's really hot. It tastes so, so good. I'd bring her her bread and everything, and go upstairs.

My mother used to make us oatmeal every morning. We used to put paper on the floor and we'd all sit on the floor and eat the oatmeal and stuff. One time, I tripped over one of my sisters and brothers and got slashed on the leg and my mother says, "You should have watched where you was going." Shoot. And they're laughing at me. I'm like, "That's alright. That's alright." It was like a point that we'd eat oatmeal and milk...they gave us powdered milk and we'd run out of it. It tasted more like carnation milk if you don't do it right. We used to have the milk with the Corn Flakes. It was more like we was making it, but barely making it.

At nighttime, too, my oldest brother and his girlfriend used to take us to Prospect Park over there on 18th between 8th and 9th. And we walked every single day to the park. It'd be dark. But it would be safe. We used to go to the zoo, go here, go there. We didn't have no problems. We didn't get stopped by the police or nothing like that. We would be walking with everybody and come back through there late at night and it was comfortable. You could fall asleep on somebody's steps or outside, and nobody'd bother you. Nobody robbed you. Nobody would touch you. It was real safe back then.

Like I said, we could barely make it home sometimes, fall asleep and you'd wake up... keep your trail going on like you're out in the woods or out in the country somewhere. But it was safe. It was a beautiful neighborhood too. Like I said, there was a church across the street. We used to play double Dutch in front of the church, hopscotch. We had a little thing next door. We used to get into arguments with people next door, back and forth with the people in the building. And it'd be crazy, because there was nobody else to argue with, so we'd argue back and forth with the people next door. But, the neighborhood be safe. We'd be out there fighting. And they'd probably be like, "Those dumb kids are fighting in the neighborhood."

We used to go to church across the street and it was a beautiful church. It had two exits and you go up and meet right up the stairs and go right into the church. It was really nice. There were doors downstairs right under the staircase that you go in for prayer and everything like that. They used to have prayers on certain nights that the black crowd used to go to.

It [our apartment] was tight. It was like... they call it a railroad house. It's straight. We had the kitchen, the living room, my mother's room, and we had a little small room, and we had this big room that goes all the way to the front. That's the room we had a full sized bed for the girls and we had a twin bed for the boys. We had a mantle piece for the chimney and we used to get scared. We use to watch this movie, "The Birds." We'd try to cover the hole up 'cuz we figured they was coming down the chimney. The boys' bed used to be next to the chimney and the full sized bed was close to the middle. Next room we had my mom's ... I guess her boyfriend, or my step-father, my little brother's father's father. They put him in that room right next to where we were. He was an old guy. We used to call him Pop.

It was three girls in one [bed] and there were three boys in the other bed. I think one of the other beds we had, it folded up. You could put a little hook around it and you could slide it around on the side, because that bed was really big.

Sonia

My so-called family

When we got to New Haven, I thought, "I can be part of a family. I can be happy." At first, I thought it was going to be true. But then all I got was a lot of criticism at first. They started talking about how I looked, my skin color… and you know how adults whisper around kids and they think the child can't understand what you're saying. But sometimes the child can understand. I remember being laughed at because of my hair. My hair was orange, because the fat lady, Chubby, died my hair orange.

It was my dad's mother and his mother's mother and she had a grown son who was staying in the house. At first it was ok. Martha, which was the great grandmother, and Anna Laura [my grandmother], she did not like me. As I look back now, either she must have had a pimp, or something, because she was a player. It's like the only time she was around the house, it was just like my dad, whenever she came it was arguing. She was yelling, calling names, wanting to beat me.

[My great grandmother], Martha, at first, was the one who would take up for me. "Stop beatin' on that child." And I got to the point, I was a runner. At one point, she would take up and the next point she'd join in. In the beginning, all I wanted was to feel the love, the hugs, to feel that I'm a part, even though I know I wasn't, of their family. I would go and try to sit in the living room when they were sitting talking and I would get, "Get outta here. You just want to be with the grown folks." I would try to say, "No. I just want some attention." So, I would leave, not crying, but on the inside crying. I was too stubborn to let them see the tears. And I would go off grumbling under my voice and wish them dead.

Then it go to a point where Anna Laura, my dad's mom, she would go from telling me I had shit colored skin, no one's ever gonna love me, whores, prostitutes. And then it got to a point where I got tired of asking and then being yelled at. She was there for a few days, and then I'd see this man and these motorcycles…and then she'd be gone for months and days at a time. And then she'd come back and I remember there was always arguing over who was the boss over me. Whenever she would come around and she would tell me to do something, I would run to Martha and she would tell her, "Stop yelling at her. You're never around. You come in and you're always yelling at the kids." But, then one thing I found funny is whenever it came to beating, I got beat by everybody in the house. Anna Laura, she was crazy. Anything she picked up she would just start swinging. It was always when I was just coming in the house, not knowing why I'm getting a beating. Either she had an extension cord or two or three switches, and wherever it hit it always left a mark. I always had long switch marks across my chest. If she wasn't beating me or yelling at me, there wasn't a childhood.

I was in Kindergarten for two or three days, 'cause I was the biggest child, little girl in the class. So they skipped me up to the first grade. That was my first time ever being in a school, 'cause I hadn't went to no school 'cause they always kept me hidden out. I'd never gone out in public or been around other kids, until the age of 7.

I was kinda happy then. You know, I was in school and starting. But, I was always, you know, they didn't really want me. My dad didn't want me and gave me to them - to these people and here these people don't even want me. I was just a check. I sat back being compared. Martha, she always babysat kids. She had a godson and there was nieces and nephews and they lived all in the same neighborhood. I would always find her being kind to other kids. Even my dad, he just came around...if I did something and they couldn't catch me 'cause I ran. To beat me they would call him. If he brought anything he took it back, like days later. He didn't give me nothing.

I tried different things, even being encouraged. I remember I was singing and one time I tried the band. There was no encouragement. "You ain't gonna be able to do that. You can't do shit." So I would start something and be gung ho about it and feel that I'm good and I would hear from the teachers, "You're real good. You have a raw natural talent." They didn't show up.

Even when it came to doing homework, I would ask for help. "No. You can do that." I got yelled at and called negative names. So, I just sat there and said, "I can do this. I can encourage myself." I can remember telling myself that all the time and feeling bad and crying on the inside at the same time.

I had to take what was given, hand-me-downs. The only time I got anything new was winter. I got a winter coat every year and like five pair of pants. I kind of do the same thing now. Now that I'm grown, and I can get what I want, I still just buy that one coat, that five pair of jeans.

I played the violin in grade school. At home, I was happy to get up to go to school and I was late every day, and I had to smoke weed every day. Before they gave me to Martha, I remember Julia, we was going to a youth center. I wanted my mom so bad. I wanted to get away from these people, cause so much was happening. I was being raped on a daily basis. When that wasn't happening, I was being beat. So, we was walking to the youth center she was smoking something. It was white. She rolled it up. I watched, 'cause she was in front of me. And she says, "Now, walk back there. I'm doing something." She lit something. I was like, "What's that? What you doin'?" I'm thinking I just want to have some fun. I want my mom. I want all these feelings. I didn't know what name to put on the feelings, but I wanted to escape. I wanted anything but what I was going through and feeling. And she was like, "Here, you want to try it?" And I was like, "Yeah." And I was hooked instantly to marijuana, cause it's like, when I took that first pull, I had that warmth. I was happy. I could smile. I didn't feel bad on the inside and I wasn't crying, because up until that point, I was crying on the inside, every day, every second. So, I felt the happy feeling. It didn't bother me what was happening and what was going on.

[By high school] Anna Laura had died. She died before I got into high school. I was so happy, God forgive me, this is going to sound cruel. But, everybody was going to the hospital, because she died of lung cancer. I was making sure. I was made to go and then they was like, "Why you want to go?" And I was like, (and I got cussed out for saying it) "I want to make sure she ain't coming back." She hated me and I want to make sure she's not coming back 'cause I want to party. My great grandma Martha was cussing me out and we were going to the hospital and everybody [was] around the bed. I can still remember the look in her eyes when she looked at me and I couldn't understand why this woman hated me so much. Even on her deathbed, dying. Something happened and she went cold. Actually, I was happy. She's gone. When she died, Martha told me stories about how she was raised and how she was abused and how she was did wrong. And I figured things is going to be better. But, when Anna Laura died, Martha turned into the wicked witch.

I got so tired of being yelled at and being called names and didn't get the attention and then I started getting it negatively. One day, I left all the lights on in the house, in her bedroom, and I knew that was her pet-peeve. I stood there laughing. I got their attention now. Everybody in the house had their eyes and was yelling. Even thought they was cursing me out, calling me names, in my mind I was like, "I got your attention." This is how I need to get your attention. That was better than nothing. I know that was wrong 'cause it was negative. To me, that was like it filled me up like I was Superwoman, Superman.

But then, after that, it got so bad till I would just literally stay out of the house. I did things just so I'd get home really, really late. I got tired of the name calling. It was like I was a child who just came along, and they dumped their child on them, and they didn't care and I was a burden to them.

So, when I got into high school I was really, really smoking weed, and at this point, I started drinking, too. I was drinking beer, Budweiser. And it helped. Somehow, I started to get the money for the weed...I might as well say prostituting, tricking, all the same thing. I was eight years old the first time I willingly did it. I didn't get [money from anyone like the other kids did], so I always used to run errands. They wanted me to do a few things and I would get paid so cheaply. I still do that today.

I was taken advantage of a lot. I can remember my great grandma Martha, I might have looked at it positively if she hadn't yelled. She was like, "why you always let people use you? Why you have to kiss their ass?" I'm beginning to not let people do that. Even now, where I live at, people take advantage of me a lot.

Every year they used to take a trip, and that's where I got my love of travelling. Every year they took a trip in November. The first snowfall, we'd be on the highway heading to South Carolina. We was down South, she had moved from Connecticut to down south when I was 16. That's when I started looking at my dad as just another man, because that's when he tried to force himself on me.

Thank God for my Aunt Zeta. She was really, really sweet. When Martha used to call names and make me feel bad, my Aunt Zeta would, when my grandmother would be sleeping or in another room, she'd come to me. She'd say, "Baby, its ok. Sometimes you gotta ignore Momma. Momma crazy." I thank God for her. It was after my grandmother pulled a gun on me for 50 cents.

I had started asking questions about brothers and sisters, where I'm from who my mom is. Every time I brought it up she got so angry with me. Every time I brought it up she'd, "Don't ever come back here, you're not a part of this family." And I'm like, "How can you say that? If they are my brothers and sisters they are a part of me. They're a part of my family. I wanna know who they are. They know my mom. I want to know what they know."

During this time, in school, what really made me feel good and give me peace was music. I was in the ensemble and that was how I got out, went different places and did different things. We sung in around different places. When we moved down South, I started singing in clubs, doing talent shows and what -not. Every time anybody had anything going I would come and sing. [One night] It was kind of raining. I was getting dressed, because I had a show to do. It was in the country in Lake City. You crossed [a big roadway] and there was a club. The house was right there. All I had to do was get dressed and walk across the road. I was told Clarence Carter was coming and wanted to hear me sing, 'cause he'd heard me sing in a different talent show.

I did the talent show and before I left, my Aunt Zeta had adopted this boy named Jubby. Once again, Jubby was so ... as far as my great grandma ma felt, he couldn't do anything wrong. And to a point, my Aunt Zeta too, cause he was sneaky. He would do stuff and he would have that innocent – he was so kind and he was so sweet and so disciplined. I was one of them if you say don't do it, I did it anyway just to piss you off to get the attention. I got tired of them being kind and so sweet. They'd go out of their way and buy for him. He did everything right. He got the straight A's and I was B – borderline C. This particular day, he was stealing and I would see him doing things and didn't say anything 'cause, "You just jealous of that boy." So I didn't say anything. So this particular day, I was on my way out the door. I think the show was like 8:00 and it was 7:00-7:30, and I was getting ready to head across, 'cause it was like the sun was setting and the evening was starting. So, she stops me and says, "Some money missing out of my pocketbook." And I'm like, "Mamma, why would I steal from you? I'm about to go do a show." Every time I did, I got paid the winnings. When I came home, I didn't give her all, but if she asked, I'd give her some. I said, "I know you'd give me a sermon first, but if I asked, you'd give it to me. Why would I steal from you?" "No, I know you took it." I said, "How much is missing?" "50 cents." I looked and said, "Grandma, I didn't do it. I didn't take your money." And I'm trying to convince her and my Aunt Zeta comes and says, "Don't say nothing, cause you know Momma's crazy." And as Aunt Zeta is saying this to me, that quick, my great grandmother Martha turned and went into the other room. As I turned to walk out the door, my great grandmother came out of that room and, "I know you took it!" And she literally pointed [a gun] at me. I said, "You want to shoot me for 50 cents?" After that, I was crying on the way across to go to the club and wiping my face in the bathroom, putting on my makeup. I did the show, got drunk and then after that I decided I was going to look for my brothers and sisters. And that's when she said, "If you leave, don't ever come back." And I never did.

Sonia
Living without

I was always that kid without. So, how I earned change for my pocket was, I used to go to the store for neighbors. They would give me, like, 50 cents and even though that wasn't enough, I was happy to get that until I was 8 years old. My great grandmother on my dad's side, her best friend's name was Ruth. Ruth was a preacher and there was someone in the family who was supposed to have been a deacon in her church. Ruth would send me to the store. My grandma would send me across the street to get stuff for Miss Ruth or if he [the deacon] wanted something from the store he would just call me.

Now, they thought he was sending me to the store. But he wasn't. I ain't never told nobody this. I would pretend like I was going to the store. I would play it off. As I look back now, I know it's so sick. But, I used to get so happy when he called 'cause I knew I would have money in my pocket. I didn't like...I hated what I had to do. But, I figured I'd have money. I didn't spend it right away so they didn't know I had money.

Every time I would ask for money I would get, "Isn't it enough that we have to feed you and clothe you?" So, after hearing that so many times, I got tired of hearing it. And then one day a lady told me, when my dad had me in hiding before he gave me to his mother's mother, she said, "Use what you got to get what you want." And I was like, "What?" And she was like, "You got a body. Use what you got down there." And I remembered that. Then when I was with Great Grandma Martha and them, the guy, whenever he would call me to go to the store, I would go to the store, 'cause I had to play it off like I was actually going to the store. But by the time I came back, it took like 45 [minutes]. I tried not to be too long. Miss Ruth, she had this big garden in the back of her house and like a shed and big bushes. I'd be lying down on the ground behind her garden. They never knew, or if she did, she never said anything.

He would give me like, sometimes it was close to $10 or sometimes it was five. It was enough to keep in my pocket. But I never let them know I had it. I did that until we moved down South when I was 17. Then when we moved down South, I didn't do that anymore, 'cause then they saw that I could sing. Once they heard that I could sing, they would ask me to play at the clubs. So, I made money doing that – singing at different talent shows. And I worked in tobacco fields. I cropped tobacco. I picked tobacco. I string tobacco. I even did cotton once. I couldn't take that. Wherever I knew I could get paid in cash, that's where I worked at.

Then, when I left South Carolina, up until I got my [casino] license, I had just had Mutia and I was jumping around from here to there, I would stay in hotels. I was tricking more. I never did the pimp thing. I refused. I couldn't see myself, it was bad enough I was already degrading myself by selling my body and then to turn around and to hand the money to a man and end up with nothing, No. I couldn't see that. I did it to keep food, to pay for a hotel. I did that for a long time, many years.

Until, after I had Jasmine. I worked for a newspaper. This was all God. I didn't have a Social Security card. But they hired me anyway. Right after that I lived in Florence, South Carolina. That's when someone told me, "If you've been here long enough, you could possibly get a Social Security card." So that's when I went down to the Social Security Department in Florence and they told me what I needed. I didn't have the I.D. I didn't have no benefit cards. I didn't have nothing. I applied for the Social Security card, and by luck, I got it. I was there long enough and they considered me a resident. I was scared when I filled the application out and I put down Florence, South Carolina. I prayed so hard, 'cause I was so scared I was going to pop up in their computer that I wasn't. It didn't, so that's how I got the Social Security card and I was able to really get jobs legit.

I had moved from there, after I had lost Mutia. Before I left South Carolina, I went into rehab. Really, the whole time I was down South, I did more street stuff 'cause I couldn't get many jobs. I used my body for a very long time to take care of myself, whether it was for food, or whether it was for drugs, money to pay for a hotel. I remember, I stayed at hotels for years, me and Mutia. When I left South Carolina, I stayed in hotels in Jersey.

Jasmine is the first [child]. Now, that's when I actually got into the drugs, after I lost Jasmine. I got pregnant when I was 18. I had her when I was 19. Then, when I really started working on the books real good, I was in Jersey. [I had] a casino license. How I got that was – that's surprising, too. They didn't ask me for no birth certificate or anything. Actually, I was working through a temp agency. I did that too, 'cause a lot of times the temp agencies didn't ask you for a birth certificate as long as you could show some type of Social Security card. They let you right in. I've never had a driver's license. First time I ever had a State I.D. is when I moved here [Albany, NY].

When I had Jasmine, I did get Food Stamps for a while there. So, I had the Welfare card. So, I'd use that when I worked in the casinos. I didn't have the state I.D., so I used the casino I.D. Even though I didn't have the State I.D., if I had some type of picture I.D., I was able to talk my way into letting me use that. I did that for a long...'till I came here.

I left the casinos and started working for ARA Food Services. I used my casino I.D. to get that. I remember I got a call. I kept having this dream that my dad's mother's mother, was dying. When I called, come to find out, she was sick. She was knocking on death's door. So, when I called, she was like, "I need you to come down and clean out my house." She knew that I'm the type of cleaner, if you ask me to clean, I'm going to clean. If you've got important papers, anybody in there, I'll kick them out, too, while I'm cleaning. That's what I did. I quit my job.

They begged me. That was the first time anyone ever begged me. My boss - I hated this name. She used to call me Red Sonia from the movie. When I left that job, she was like, "Wow, you're leaving just when I'm about to promote you." I was working as second cook under the head chef. I never went to school, just got the job and learned a lot and started moving up and she was about to make me under the head chef. I was like, "I have to go."

So, I got down South. Three days after I got there, thank God I did go, her heart was skipping 3-4 beats at a time. She ended up having a stroke. I cleaned her house out. She was five months behind in everything. I ended up getting back into the streets again, because I didn't have money to take care of myself. So, I got involved with drug dealers. Mutia's dad, he don't even know he has a daughter. But, after I was there, caught up all her bills, she was five months behind in everything. So, I cleaned it up. Then, her stepson came up there and they took her back to Connecticut. I was blamed for everything that was wrong, her bills... I was the one who was blamed. I was the one who burned down the house. And I had nothing to do with it. So, they left me stranded in South Carolina.

So, I'm like, "Ok, no money, no place to stay." I reverted back to selling myself. Then, that's when I met... and I'm somewhat still ashamed of this, 'cause I never really knew his name. I just knew him by, he was a drug dealer. At the time, I was tricking with him. He took care of me, 'cause they left me literally stranded in the woods and in Lake City, South Carolina, that's the woods. I had no car, nothing. The house, which was my great grandmother's daughter's house, she wanted to leave it to me. But they made a big fuss because, Martha wanted to leave it to her son, Benny. So, I was like, "I don't want nothing nobody wants me to have." My Aunt Zeta was like, "Thank you for the thought. But to keep the peace, go ahead and give it to your mom." And that's what she did. When they left, even though the house was hers and her son's, the son called the police. They had the police escort me out of the house.

What I did to get back at them, being I was homeless and in the streets, in the woods, no place to stay, I sold everything in the house. That was wrong. I was crying every time I sold anything, even the house, but I couldn't do that, cause it wasn't mine. So, after that, that's when I met Mutia's dad, the drug dealer. His name was Santa Claus. I know. I went through a doozie with that name in court. So, for a while, if it weren't for him... We stayed in a house. Every day he would put money in my pocket, every week to make sure I was taken care of. Then, I decided I was going to rehab. No, I found out I was pregnant. I broke up with him because I got tired. I didn't want to continue to live like that. Then, I found out I was pregnant and the guy I was with, I'm five months pregnant with Mutia, he was supposed to have been my fiancé, we bought a new house in South Carolina and he got a hooker in the house.

So, I ended up and drinking and just going really crazy then. I'd say it was crazy, gave birth to Mutia and the whole time I thought it was the guy Ronald I was with. It wasn't until after I had the blood test and we went to court, 'cause his mother kept saying, "That's not your daughter. That's not your daughter." He was claiming her and taking care of her. When we went to court, you know when you see them on Jerry Springer, I didn't take it that far, I was like, "Oh my God, I made a mistake." By that time, I didn't know where [Santa Claus was], 'cause he had two nicknames, one was Santa Claus and one was Snowflake. That's because he was like the kingpin down there. He was like, if you were hungry and you was an addict, he'd give you money. He'd feed you. That's how he got the name. So, by that time, I had no clue where he was at, didn't know his first name. The day I was going to tell him I was five months pregnant, I found out he was married with five kids somewhere in Florida. So, I was like, "He don't need to know. He already got five children. How he gonna do for mines?" I stayed there for a little while longer, got clean.

What happened was, even after I got clean, I had Mutia. I did good for a while. I moved from Lake City to Sumpter, South Carolina. Everything was good. When she grew, I found myself jealous. I don't know to call it jealous, but I found myself wanting what my child had. Some days it was so hard for me to even pick her up. As strong as those feelings got, and I was scared to talk to anybody, cause I didn't really know anybody and I was afraid they were gonna try to take her from me. So, I just started, I wasn't drinking, I was doing good. I wasn't doing nothing but smoking cigarettes. It was so strong, this feeling that I couldn't take it. So, I went and got a Budweiser and I started drinking again. That first drink just, after that I was like I couldn't take it. I just started getting high again. I was so afraid, 'cause I didn't want to lose her, and I knew deep down what I was doing. And I was working. This was another thing. The way I got our apartment we were staying in, I was working for Polite Real Estate. The woman was out of the military and I trusted her. She owned her own house, had a home based business. I did her advertising. I did it on foot, handing out business cards, flyers. They did second mortgages. I even did the contracts, set up the appointments...never got paid though. She ended up using me, dogged me -never seen a paycheck.

So one day, it was these church people, this particular day, I was pulling a trick. I had the side apartment. You could come up on the porch and my bedroom window was right there, and you walked past my window to get to the front door. I forgot the window was open. Mutia's room was on the other side. If I had company, I made sure Tia was in the bed asleep before I was doing anything. This particular day, I thought Mutia was sleeping. I was giving a man head. Mutia, I did not see her at the foot of the bed. She was standing there all bright eyed. I was trying to hurry up and jump up and the lady from the church, she stuck her head in the window. She seen and she yelled, "Look at that baby!" and I'm like, "Mutia!"

Weeks went by, days went by. I had stopped the tricking because I had gotten so scared. Then the police showed up at the door, saying that someone reported me. And I know exactly who did. So, they took her and that's when all the court started. I got clean. I tried my best to stay clean while I was there. But there was no work, nothing for me to do. So, I left, 'cause I was in recovery. I had moved to Charlotte. Everything was going good. I was back and forth doing the visits and spending time with her. Then, I met someone in Charlotte. I was living in Charlotte, but he was here. He was like, "Come to New York." So, I was like I could possibly live a little bit better - have my daughter transferred there.

The first five years, even though I've been here 13, I don't count the first 5, because every other month I was down South. I was here, but I wasn't really, really settled because I was back and forth. I was trying to get her transferred here. Their whole goal was bringing us back together, only to find out, I went through eight caseworkers. Five of them quit. When I say I was doing everything they asked me to do, I did everything. But then, in the end, while they're telling me they wanted to give her back to me, they never had any idea. The guardian testified for me, the foster parent testified on my behalf and the judge, said to me, "Ms. Graham, I commend you. You have changed your life. I do believe you are ready to be a mother to your child, but I'm taking account of your past and I'm judging you because you have a terminal illness." I sat there and I'm like, "What?" And he said, "Well, do you want to see her?" And I said, "No, I do. But, I don't want my child's last memory of her mother to be you all pulling her away, she's hollering, screaming and crying and no one can give her an explanation why." I decided, "She's in school. She's happy. She's learning. That's how I want her to continue. I don't want her to have no emotional hang-ups." So, then they set up what was, a new home. Even then I wasn't working. I didn't have an income then, either. I was still off and on, for a long time the way I took care of myself was I sold my body.

Before I moved here [Albany], I had gotten married. That ended three weeks after I got married. But during that time, two of the church ladies, they had started a Social Security thing for me. After the marriage thing didn't work, that's when I moved to Charlotte. I went into supported living, had copped a job for this TV station. It was a talk show. I was, like, working under the host. And just before I left, she had talked to me about working on the show. They had done this one segment on HIV and how it is. That's when I first started doing outreach work.

So, I left and I moved up here, 'cause that's when I met Jonathan. Mentally, in my mind, I'm like maybe life can be a lot better. I can come up and make something of my life. I got into a program and I had to get set up, because of DSS and the Foster Care Unit. I was working and had gotten a therapist. It was the first time I had went in to therapy since I was younger in Jersey. My first caseworker up here, helped me to actually get an income. Now, I say he was sent by God, because he was there long enough to help me get my Social Security and he just moved out of state.

The State of New York, I saw their doctors and talked to their lawyers, I don't like to claim what they said, 'cause they took it as far as Borderline Personality Disorder and PTSD. I was so chronically depressed. The best thing I can describe it as [like] the vets.

Gloria
Coming of age

So, I think I was in the fourth grade then. You should have seen me. I told my mother, I said, "You got to buy me one of those things with the balls on it." And she said, "What is that?" She said, "That's like a baby thing." I said, "No, it's not. That helps me out a lot [in math class]." She wouldn't get it either. I used to do English and tried to read about Dick and Jane and Sally. And I was like, "That's a nasty name in that book. I'm not reading that!" We'd go through the whole thing. They got us all with the books and I couldn't read it. I couldn't understand. So they said, "Look at the picture. What do you see?" I see the boy and the girl and stuff like that. They're riding a bike or playing ball or playing with the dog. I don't know what the dog's name is. But, I know it was Dick and Jane back then. I think it was the only two names they had in the book.

It was really crazy, 'cuz as I went from one grade to the other, I ended up going to the same grade with this one girl. She used to pick at me. She used to always push me, wanna fight me. I be walking to school, coming from school, and then the public school graduated and everything. And I couldn't go on trips 'cuz I didn't have no money...they always say we go to the Statue of Liberty, we go here we go there. I never had the money. So, I never had a chance to visit all those things in the city that I grew up around. I still haven't been to the Statue of Liberty. I'll go one day.

After that, I think, I finally graduated [from 6th grade] ... this particular time, I think, we went to see Fiddler on the Roof. My father came over and he gave me the money to go. So, it was on a Saturday. When that was done with, our mothers were supposed to meet us back at the school. This one girl came back over there and started pushing on me, hitting me. And I said, "I am so tired. I'm so tired. I'm so tired." I finally turned around and punched her right in her face and flipped her and everything. Next day, we got her mother. So, I had to call my mother. My mother said, "My daughter been gettin'- your daughter been picking at my daughter for a long, long time. I guess she's tired." Like that. I was just so happy. I was like, "I finally went ahead for it." My mother used to tell me, "You're so scared. You let you sister fight and everything. You're not supposed to leave your sisters."

I was like 10 or 11 years old. I think it was about 11. It was sixth grade. I went to Junior High School, then I went to the annex of this other school. It was really terrible. It was in this neighborhood. It's East New York. Pennsylvania Avenue. Over there, that school had everything. It had so much going on, because what happened was, they gave everybody a choice to go to whatever high school they want to, if their grades were to a certain level. If you're grades were up to a certain level, you have a choice of schools you want to go to. If your grades were not there, you just made it over that borderline, you're ok. Also, I was getting good at math, but the reading and all that other stuff, I wasn't good at. What happened was, they told me, "Well you're going to this school." Like that. And I was like, "That's fine. As long as I went on." [They said], "Because of the fact of you come in and you take the test and everything, but then you leave." I didn't want to stay there. I didn't have clothes. It was at a point I had one bra, one panty and they was ripping up. Every time school starts, I didn't have anything. I felt so embarrassed. I used to borrow this girl's clothes and everything. It got to a point, the girl moved. I didn't have anything. She wasn't about to give me her clothes and everything like that. So, back then, I didn't know anything about the thrift shop and second hand stores. I never knew nothing about that. So, I would go myself. But nobody knew back then. My mother didn't bring us out around anybody else. If she was going anywhere, we used to go to church way in Harlem. It was on the train. It would take us out to Harlem. [She'd] get us dressed. It was like a big old roller, about this long (gestures), and [she]wrapped my hair around this big old spongy, crunchy roller and give us a little bang that was way back here. We used to wear them ugly stockings - those brown stockings. She used to put those brown stockings on us. Back then, I don't even think we know what tights was, 'cuz it was cold and we had none on. So when we went to church we had the brown stockings on.

But we didn't get a chance to visit nothing. We didn't go to the zoo. The only time we got to go to the zoo was when my bother, my oldest brother, took us to the zoo, Prospect Park. My mother, the only time she took us out was always to buy a loaf of bread, Wonder Bread and some bologna and some other stuff... the cheese to go on a barbeque, or whatever it was. We didn't call it a barbeque at that time. We called it a picnic back then. We didn't call it a barbeque. So, we'd go on our picnic and stuff, and from there she used to go visit her mom and we were that small.

I remember I was about 10 or 11 years old. I remember we would always get on this train that took us all the way down South. You could sleep in it, but you have to pay more money if you sleeping up in those little curtain things. We used to all be sitting up in there and squished in our seats, going down South. Now, that was a long ride. We used to go down there and my grandmother didn't have no running water. She didn't even have a bathroom. We used to go outside to some outhouse in the woods. At night, we used to have a bucket in the house. But, at night, if you had to go really bad and do number two, you go outside to the outhouse.

And when we'd get the water, there's a certain path to get the water to get to the well. Or, you'd get these things all stuck in your socks, your legs, everything. I don't know what they called those, but it was really crazy. We used to have to put the bucket on a hook. A few times, it ended up getting off the hook and it fell off. Then, you had to figure out a way to get it hooked back on to the thing to bring the water up. Drop it down in there, and bring it back up, and bring it in the house. And we used to do water like that. We had one of those stoves you open up and put the fire in and stuff like that. And then when they locked the door, they put this big piece of wood behind the door and you can't see nothing outside. I said, "I'm not sleeping near the window, 'cuz you can't see. What happens if a bear comes or something? No, no, no."

Then, my mother had me out there picking cotton, too. With this big bag - it looked bigger than me, put it around my shoulder. Itchy, itchy thing, as you're going down the way to pick the cotton, about 10 or 11 years old. We'd get up at 4:30 in the morning. My thing is, they'd cook breakfast and everything. I'm like, "How you all cookin' breakfast at 4:30 in the morning?" You had to be healthy to go out there and pick that cotton. They said the reason why they get up so early…when the sun come out, you roast. That's why they wear the big hats, so the sun don't get all in their face and stuff. I started running through there tripping over stuff and a woman said, "What you trip over?" And I said, "A watermelon." And she said, "Go get that watermelon. That's yours." I was like, "For real?" And I ended up with a watermelon. But, they never told me there were snakes and stuff out there, 'cuz I'm a child. I don't think about that stuff. But there was a certain time they come out. I was rushing through the woods and then this brown stuff was closed up and then it opened up. I used to think it was cotton candy. But, what makes it so bad is when you're picking it, the bag don't look like it never gets full. Never. You got to be out there like four or five hours picking cotton, then you take a little break and finish. It'd be like maybe 12:00 and you'd get your biscuits and the beans and all that stuff.

Then right next to the house is a corn field. I didn't like that, you get lost in that. I'd never see them go in and get no corn. I had no corn. I'm like, "What's wrong with the corn? Nobody eating the corn!" Then I started looking at that movie, "Children of the Corn." I'm like, "Come on, this is crazy."

They gave us a choice of the schools we could go to. It seemed like they called all the people and had them fill out papers and I didn't get one. So, one of my girlfriends said, "Why you didn't get one?" And I said, "Because of the fact that I haven't been coming to school," and I'd been passing the tests, just barely passing the tests. And they said, "Well you're good at math." And I said, "My English and that stuff is not great." I didn't know at that time what was bothering me. I can do stuff real good, if I'm there a length of time and somebody show me constantly and I do it instead of them - instead of doing it for me. I'm quick learner once I keep doing it over and over again, while that person helping me. But, for some reason...it's crazy. The school part is the same thing. I used the excuse that everybody came to school all nice and clean and beautiful things and their hair done. I was embarrassed. The kids said, "You're in the [8th grade] graduation." But my father didn't get me no clothes. He didn't get me anything.

By that time, when I went to graduate, I had left my mother's house when I was 13. My mother was an alcoholic. She already had cirrhosis of the liver. Back then, I didn't even know what high blood pressure was. She used to catch seizures. We didn't know what to do. We used to rush out of the house and knock on some person's door and tell them my mother's shaking on the floor and all this stuff. They said, "Turn her sideways and put something in to hold her tongue." We said, "For what?" And they said, "So she don't swallow her tongue." I didn't ever know what that was. After all that, my mother wouldn't stop drinking. She'd have all these seizures. I said, "Come on!"

Finally, when my step-father gets there, he's arguing and fighting with her and beating her up and all that stuff. He says she's drinking and stuff. It's to a point where my mother had a bottle under the mattress, one in the bathroom under the sink. She had one in the kitchen under the sink and we didn't think nothing of it. Then, she used to make it! She used to get these peaches, some yeast and some other stuff and put it under the sink and let it sit there.

She met up with another boyfriend, I guess, and she broke up with my little brother's father. And he fought her and beat her up. So, she took us and left and took us to the other boyfriend's house. He had something like a railroad house and he had a big dog called Rex. He didn't like kids neither. They used to put him down in the basement and that was down in part of downtown Brooklyn. This was Bourbon Street and 5th Avenue. We used to live there. It was the five of us. I had to be about 13. I had to take the bus back to school. I think I was 12. It was about the 8th grade. I left my mother when I was 13 or 14.

I went to Brownsville. It was crazy. It was a neighborhood, I'd never seen so many black people, 'cuz I'd been in a neighborhood with a lot of white people at the time. My brother talked me into going. He said, "Mommy gotta go to the hospital." But I waited it out a little while and stuff like that. But then, I used to go with my mother to the bootlegger. It's two blocks down from where she used to live at. And the guy is always talking about, "Can I talk to your daughter?" And my mom, "Is you crazy? She's only 12 or 13!" And my mother used to...the scary part was, she used to get the empty bottles and tell me to take it down to the guy. I used to go there to give him the bottles to put the liquor in the bottles... and it'd be a Sunday and you can't be selling. But I used to bring it home to her and he used to try to talk to me. I was so scared of him. Oh, God, here were go. This man want to touch me. I'm not going through this. So, what happened, I got the bottles for her and the next day, my brother said, "You ready to go?" and I said, "Yeah. I don't know what's going on. That guy keeps trying to talk to me." And he already knew what happened to me back when I was about 9 or 10 years old.

My step-father came in there and was touching me and my sister. He told us we better not say nothing. At that time, I ran away when he did it. I took off out the door. I had my little granny dress on - little house on the prairie dress on. I don't know where I ran. But I was getting ready to tell my mother he pushed me and knocked me down. My mother said, "What is it you're about to tell me?" I said, "He pushed me and knocked me down." And I took off and ran out the door. I got on a train going to Coney Island, but it was pouring down rain. I kept going to different train stops. I kept getting on the train. Finally, this guy came up to me and said, "You alright?" I just shook my head and thank God he wasn't a crazy person. And he said, "You know what? I'll take you home to my wife." He took me home. They had a beautiful house. I ate and everything. They washed me up, put me in some clothes and everything. Then, they asked me what police station is by my house. They said if nobody had reported you, you could stay with us. But they called the police station and my mother was there. So, they said, "We got to take you home." They said,

"You can spend the night. But we got to take you home tomorrow." So, they ended up taking me home.

My mother was still with the other person. So I waited. My brother said, "What you want to do?" I didn't know what to do. I was only 10 years old. So, I was about…it happened again. It was like each year. My brother took me and moved to his house in Coney Island. When I got to Coney Island, my brother said he was going to meet me in the area. When I got there, his girlfriend's father was there. And he said, "Well, your brother's upstairs." And I said, "Why he won't come down?" And he said, "I'm going to run upstairs and lock the door. Come on." That's when I went upstairs with him and he closed the door behind me and he had a knife and that that's when that happened to me then, too. So, finally when I went to leave out, I ran out the door. And it's nothing but Italian people in the area. I'm like, "I'm a little black girl…" Like why is she whatever? So, finally I told my brother what happened and he went looking for him and I don't know what happened. But he told me I would be alright.

He [my brother] passed away when I was 18. He worked in the hospital with the physical therapists. For some reason, back then, they wasn't putting the sharpies in a sharp container. They had it in something else. He got stuck with a needle. He ended up with meningitis. It was crazy. He didn't know what was the consequences behind it, so whoever he was around, we all had to get a shot. So, we're screaming and crying and when we went to see him, we had to wear masks. It got really bad. He was in Kings County Hospital. He used to work in this other hospital down on 6th Street…Methodist Hospital in Brooklyn. Once he got stuck, he stayed in the hospital off and on, off and on, off and on. Every time we went to visit him, we had to wear masks. But we had to go to the Health Department and get shots. We ended up getting shots and everything.

We went to visit him. I went to visit him the most, because I was close to him. He explained to me, "When you go to Kings County Hospital for anything, don't stay there, 'cuz they will cut you up for anything." And that's what he said. "They cut me up looking for something and all it was was my legs swelling up." And he showed me his stomach, and he was cut up all kinds of ways. I don't know what they was looking for, and back then I didn't understand. So, he passed away after that.

My other brother [Ronnie] told me, "Come on. I think we should go now." We called him Bubba. When all that stuff happened, he had a lot of stress going on and stuff. Every time we did something, he used to make us stand on one foot with our arms in the air and we couldn't move. If we was bad, he used to sit us in the corner, like we was in school or something, and we couldn't move. If we turned around, he'd punch us. So, what happened, since I was my mother's favorite, every time he went to punch me, I'd be like, "I'm a tell...I'm a tell!" No. No. No. I had a lot of fun with him before he passed. He passed away when he was 21.

[Before that, when I was 13] I went to another area with my step-mom. She puts me in school and everything. I go to school. I pass and everything, like I said. I didn't get a choice of where I'm going to go. I was in Brownsville, Ocean Hill. I went to school...I got a summer job. And the summer job was over there in these two buildings: 510 and 514 Howard Avenue, between St. John's and Sterling. I was in Brownsville, Ocean Hill – that part of Brooklyn that is terrible. Back then the thing was dope. Everyone was high with dope, cuz' it was the 60's then. They used to have one building on the corner. They'd be on the roof, they'd be everywhere. But they dressed. They could dress their behind off. I used to live across the street and they had those two buildings and there was a lot of black people there and my father was the super there. So, I stayed with them.

Sonia

The "System"

I always tried to shy away from those [HIV] programs. Like Whitney
Young is a program. They have different programs to teach you how to
keep up on the different medicines, how to stay healthy. I took this one
class dealing with people with chronic disorders. But, I really tried to stay
away. That was one of the ways that I could cope. I know people, but as
far as groups - I used to [go to groups], but then I stopped because I
didn't trust them. When I came outside, I would hear what was said in
the groups. It got to the point, even on Green Street, that's why I can't
wait to move from there. One of the things I would have to deal with,
before someone meets me, before they even get to know me, it's like
what I'm hearing. So, I guess as a way to protect myself, I figure if they
don't see me with other people, the less they know.

I did cleaning. I worked at the bank for a while. For a long time, I did the
cleaning on my own. I did enjoy it because, I had money. I could do
things. I didn't have to worry about running out. I had money coming in.
But the other part was, I was really being shafted by the client, too. They
was under paying me. That was one of my mistakes. When I first started,
and I researched, they charged $60 – I'll charge $30. But it was supposed
to be an hour, not $30 a day. When I tried to correct that, "Oh I can't
afford it." One of the things I learned in business is you have to be a little
shrewd. You can be kind, but not so, so, kind, because then they'll take
that and run. That's what ended up happening. [I did the cleaning] until I
had to go back in that brace again. One winter, I fell in a pothole. Then, I
couldn't do it no more. When I came home, after I used to get done doing
her house, I would stop and catch the bus on the corner of Quail. I was
shopping, and I fell into the pothole, and I ended up in the brace.

I did that for a couple of years. I was beginning to get more business, but
what stopped me was, one, transportation and two, I wasn't bonded. So,
I stopped while I wasn't on my feet.

The pitfalls for me, I was gung ho about computers. But, when it was time to do it, it was like, I don't know. I'm so tired of feeling like I haven't succeeded in anything. So, I don't know. Is it that I've gotten comfortable?

I have skills, but not really mastered them. I haven't been to work in a while, so that puts me where there are so many people ahead of me. I would have to take the mediocre jobs, probably won't be any benefits, because when you're working part-time there is no benefits. Or, when you take the lesser jobs, there may be some, but they don't kick in until a certain time. And then with certain companies, there are none. [Not having medical benefits] wouldn't be good at all, because then I wouldn't be able to get the medicine. I'd have to keep dealing with Welfare and I really don't want to deal with them. It's like, it's bad enough that a person, they may not be in a position in life that they want to be in and then they gotta deal with DSS. I always felt shameful having to deal with DSS.

I hide the fact that I have a brace on my foot, because of them thinking oh, I have a liability or not getting hired because of that. It's the income. As soon as you started out and they get wind of it, they gonna cut it. I don't mind. I would love to come off of disability. I'm not gonna sit here and lie, 'cause right now it is my income. Without it, I wouldn't have one. That's why I thank God, because I'd probably be out there selling my body just to make ends meet. That's one thing I promised I was not going back to.

[The PTSD] makes me feel like a failure sometimes, because I see other people. They have their careers, they're thriving, meaning, you know, they went to school, they're working in a field that they want to. And they're making the money to take care of them and their family. When you're on disability, it's very little. It's almost like Welfare, but it's not. [Living in subsidized housing], at first, I didn't have any problem being around the drug addicts, the dopers, cause its cheaper rent. You can pay your rent and still have a little bit to pay some bills and still have a little bit left over. But then, at the same time, it's not really all that good, 'cause it's so much mess around it. It's like, if you're a person changing your life and you're coming from, you know, just living on the streets and doing them things you do on the streets, the hustling, being around the dopers the manipulation and all that, when you change your life and you're still living around all them people, it's like, ok, I'm not doing it no more. I am better than this. But, at the same time, I'm still here. Am I really? But you know you are. But, then again that's the only place you can afford.

I've been thinking about [getting another apartment], but thing is being able to afford it. I can't afford...my rent's only $204 now. I can pay that. I can pay my light bill and the phone, and send some off for charity and still have a little money in my pocket. But lately, I've been thinking I really want to move, so I can have the peace and...but, that would mean my rent would be. [My total income is] $20-$30 from being $800. My rent was $525, nothing included, before I moved into housing [15 years ago]. I found myself, after I paid rent, I paid the lights, cable phone, there was no money for me or for the house. So, I looked to the streets. And that was wrong. So, that was one reason I went back to school. I'll get a diploma, but that's where I'm messing up. I find myself getting into things, like the computers. Back in Atlantic City, I went to ACC for computer operation. I thought I was gung ho. But, once I learned and I graduated and got the job, I had no clue what to do. I mean, I actually did the program...and then I wasn't enthusiastic about it. So, I just quit that job.

So when I went to Austin's, once again, for the cosmetology, then, I found myself not liking it, after I got into it. It's no problem going back, taking the test and I think the test part of it, too. I don't like tests. This will be my eighth time [taking the GED test]. Comprehension is not the thing. I comprehend very well. I'm not even going to sit and blame it on the weed. It's not that. I honestly think it's the test thing, cause even if I think back... I really haven't succeeded at much, or could have been always hearing growing up, I didn't stop hearing till I was like 17 and I really got out on my own that I could do. You know, the encouragement. So, I've always had to give it to myself. But, then I was always lacking whenever I needed to really, really push. Ok, you can do this no matter what. At times, it's just hard. I just give up and don't believe that I can do it, when this is something I want to do. A lot of times that voice be so loud, "You can't do this. You're gonna fail."

I don't hardly ever talk about it [PTSD and depression]. I cry at least once a day. I hide a lot. I don't want to tell anyone. A lot of times, I get this strong feeling like, I want my mom. I want my mom. Like now, when I'm going through different things in life, it gets so strong. I want my mom. I'll just either smoke more weed or drink more. I remember when I was six and started smoking the weed and started drinking and it actually was like Tylenol. But, now, it's getting to the point where it ain't nothing but a habit now. It doesn't work anymore, because I can smoke a Dutch and it's like I have to smoke a whole lot to really drown it out. And I'm not willing to do that no more. I'm just smoking and still be depressed. So that's why I'm like, it's time to look for a different avenue. If I'm blessed enough to find [my mom's] grave and say my goodbyes and let it go. But then who wants to wait? What if I never find it? I know I have gotta have some way to make peace with it. But, I have to somehow, and I have no clue.

Sonia

The Housing Trap

The benefits of [subsidized housing] is that the rent is cheap. It's the cheapest in the state. You can, say if you're a single person, or if you're on a monthly income, you can pay your rent, pay your bills and have some monies left over to play with. Once you get in there, it's not all that cheap, because if you're working, that's where it will do you in. They're constantly raising the rent. If you're on social services or social security, your rent'll stay the same. But, then the flip side of that, after you get done paying the rent and all the different fees the outrageous prices they charge you for little things like blinds. I understand they gotta have a fee if you lose your keys or something. But if, say, you lock your keys in the house...it's not like they're changing the locks, they're just turning a master key and they're charging $50-$60 for that.

Then on top of that, if you're a person not that used to so many people around you, that can be...on one hand you're not lonesome. But then again, they're nasty, disrespectful, nosey. Nosey is not the word. You have privacy, 'cause you got your own apartment, but then there isn't any privacy. The walls are like paper thin. You've got people over you. There's no consideration for people living under you. It tends to get nerve wracking all the time, people knocking on your door asking for this...everybody's living too close.

I've never felt safe in that building. I've had a fear of heights [living on the 12th floor and now the 6th]. But not just because of the fear of heights. It's if anything were to happen, if you're on the lower floors, you're good. But if there was a real bad, bad fire and I'm scared the building will blow up, cause there's people in there on oxygen and people be smoking in the hallways. It's getting dangerous now, people's done got stabbed up in the building. So, it's like, it's not all that safe anymore, 'cause when you come out your door, you gotta make sure you either got something in your hand, or make sure there's nobody sleeping out there in front of your door, in the hallways. So, at one point it was safe. But now it's not, 'cause you got some of everything in there and everybody doing stuff in the building.

You know how when you go to motor vehicle, you gotta sit in line and wait? Well, on some days on certain floors...ain't nothing but drug dealing going on. From the time you wake up, and they got so slick with it – they don't do it during the daytime no more. They come in at night and especially the first of the month, you got the ones that smoke crack hanging in the hallway. Even young people be in the stairwell screwing. I don't know how many times, I've been like, "Come on. Go on home across the street. Why do you all come over here? You ain't makin' no babies over here." You got the men in the hallway smoking crack or shootin' up dope. It's like, any given time there's condoms on the floor, or you come out and there's blood on the wall. It's disgusting. And then, on top of it, there are grown people peeing. You can't even walk down the stairwell...You talking 'bout you want the tenants to do something about it? Come on. At the end of the night these people got guns. They're dealing in heroine and drugs. Every time they fix the locks, they're breaking the locks at night, so they can get in to get the dope or get in to sleep. On one hand, it started out being nice, 'cause you got your own – you ain't got to live with nobody. But then that saying, "God bless the child that got its own."

Trying to live someplace else, you know you got your money, you got kind of a budget where you can pay the bills. But, then again, part of me is like I'd rather go back to... before I was living in Housing I was paying almost $525 a month with nothing included. I still have enough now, but the rent is less than $200, so I'm like, "Yay." But I had more privacy in an apartment than here. And it's constantly, someone is doing this...and when I say nosey – people's all in your business when they got no business. So on one hand, it's a lot of drama that goes on here.

I mean [if I moved], I find, someone I just spoke to, he has a one bedroom cottage. He's charging $300 a month for it. I was like, "I can do that. I can pay the first month's rent and security." That's $600 out of my check and won't have to go to DSS for nothing. But I'm like, if it's not bigger than what I'm in now, ain't no need to move into it. So, he was saying that was coming open in June. I was thinking about that 'cause I won't have no one over me. It's a whole house. But, then the flip side of that, it's kind of on my conscience is, the person's married and I know he likes me. So, I'm going to tell the truth, shame the Devil, cause he like me I'm like, "You shouldn't get it." When I say I'm living a different way, I'm totally living a different way. I didn't let go all the other sugar daddies to start something new with someone else. So, I'm trying to wait on Section 8. I just hope, I had gotten it two times before, but I turned it back in, because I couldn't really walk to find the apartments. So, I'm waiting for them to open the list. I'm hoping and praying that I'll be one of the next batch of letters they send out and then I'll be moving out. Other than that, I'll just have to find something that has electric included in the rent. 'Cause I'm always scared in that building.

Gloria

Starting again

Bubba didn't pass away, let me think now. I'm trying to think now, he had to pass away...when he passed away, I was pregnant. So it had to be before that [my other brother], cause I was only like 13 or 14 years old when I was with my brother Bubba and we lived in Coney Island. And then, I went back home, it's really confusing. But, I know I was pregnant during the time, and I know I ran away from home before my brother passed away. Me and Ronnie, we was with my mother in downtown Brooklyn and she was drinking. Everyone else done left. They done took my other brothers and sisters to foster homes, so it was just me and Ronnie. And he was like, "Well let's go and go to step-mom's house." And I said, "I ain't goin' nowhere, cause I'm scared to go, you know, run away. " He says, "C'mon. Mommy drinking. She ain't gonna know anyway." We ended up running away and we went to my step mom's house.

I didn't have nice clothes and stuff, so I didn't go to school like I was supposed to be going. So, I was with her, took care of the kids, cooked and everything. I got up early in the morning and cooked and all that stuff. It was so funny, I had no extra clothes. I had no underclothes. I had to wash the same ones I had on and after a while I think after a year or two...two or three years after that, what happened was, my mother passed away. After my mother passed away, I had my kids already. I was 19 when I had my first one. I think [I was] about 25...26.

One of my sisters, and us were going back and forth to the hospital, because of the fact that through the years she was, how you do you say it- a battered mother. She was always gettin' beat up by her boyfriends, because she drank and stuff like that. And every time she's with a boyfriend, she ends up getting beat up. So, this one particular time, the guy beat her up and pushed her down the steps. She had a safety pin on her eye and all this stuff. And we went in there to see her and then we were supposed to come back the next day. I went to get my brother

Ronnie, so he could see her. Before we even got there, they called us up and said she died.

It was a head injury...she had stitches all up here [around the head]. She already had cirrhosis of the liver, but they didn't know 'till after the autopsy. She wasn't drinking. We had a birthday party for her on November 6. We used to think her birthday was the 20th of November and we used to always try to celebrate it then. But when she stopped drinking, we celebrated it November 6th and she died in December.

[The boyfriend] left and went to Baltimore, Maryland. My younger sister went crazy. She said, "My mother's not dead." 'Cause she had sweat on her. I was like, "Boy, she must have just passed away. " 'Cause we went down to the morgue, it was St. Mary's Hospital in Brooklyn and we looked at our mother. And you know, you don't want to believe your parents died. I'm like, "Why's she sweating? You all just brought her down here...you sure she's not just unconscious?" I'm trying to look at her nose trying to see. Everyone's looking and my sister started jumping and she said, "She's sweating!" She was 15 or 14, at that time she didn't have no kids or anything, oh she did, she had a son and she was staying with my mother off and on out in Brooklyn. I'm like, "Ok." It was really crazy. My mother told me, 'cause we were all going through the same thing with the guys that we dated. Same exact thing, we grew up with her, seeing her get beat up all the time. And I said, "Well, how do these men know that we go through this, here? I don't tell nobody somebody's beating my mother up." But, we all were going through it. Even I was going through it. My sister, she used to get beat up by her boyfriend and used to be up there at my mother's house...she'd be arguing with him and stuff. And the same thing was happening to me, too. It's really crazy to see this go through each generation, 'cause my daughter goes through it. My younger daughter was going through it, but I said, "Don't be no punk, either he gotta go, or he ain't got no job – even if he got a job, he's still not supposed to put his hands on you. " She turned it around.

I don't be with nobody. I broke out of a relationship with someone. He was real nice. He was kind and stuff. That was back in 2004, 2003, cause I've been away from him for almost 4 years now. He was a military person. He never told me that when he was in the military, I forgot what he called it, paranoid or bugged out, or something. And the way he took care of that, if he didn't take his medication – he took drugs. If he stopped the medication, he had to find something else. He didn't let me know... exactly you know, that he was really into it. When we first met, he said, "I haven't been messing with drugs. I'll take my medication. I'm a good person." We got along really good. We went out. We went on vacation. We went shopping, we traveled a lot. I moved into his house and he kept saying, "Give up your apartment." I said, "Uh, uh. No, no, no, no, no. Uh, uh. I don't know. Then, after a year and a half two years, I didn't want him to stay with me 'cause I had girls. So, he got his own apartment and the crazy thing was, that every time he needed to use my car, I would go to work. He would get the car and drive around all day with his friends. And it was crazy, because he was very smart and very intelligent.

But my point was, he just had so much on his mind about a lot of stuff that went on. His mother passed away, his father live in North Carolina, his sister in the Bronx. But every time something happened, he would talk and talk and then he was like, "You don't pay attention to me, you don't act like a wife." I was like, "Excuse me, you're still married. I'm not married. You're still married to your two sons' mom. When you go down to the city to visit, you go stay there." "I don't stay with her." I said, "Yes, you do. Where's your son stay at?" "He stays with her, but I don't stay there." "I don't have no complaints. Don't bring nothing back to me and don't bring no bull s to me." And he would always come back and tell me about the jokes and stuff, I'd be like, "That's fine. But I'm going out. I'm not reporting to you like I'm a child. I'm a grown woman." And it got to a point where he'd say, "You have to call me and let me know this and let me know that." And I'm like, "Oh, no." And he'd say, "When you're not with me and you're not doing nothing with me, who are you with?" I'm like, "Excuse me? I already told you when we first met. I don't love you, and I'm not into this sexual thing." I'm not into women. I'm in Menopause. I'm not blaming it on the Menopause, it's just that a lot that goes on in my life, it just turns me off. I just feel numb. I just don't feel like being bothered. So, he gets upset with me. My thing was, he'd take medication. It'd be like heart medication, blood pressure medication. I wasn't trying to down him. He just can't perform. If you can't perform, and I don't want it anyway, we both was up some kind of shit creek!

He used to get so pissed off and I didn't like it. I couldn't take it. Every time he talked to me, my stomach turned. I used to get sick. You know what happened? I ain't trying to say he's short, but he's right here. He's always talking smart. He's a very smart, intelligent man, but I said, "Don't down me, because of the fact that you're this." He come out and say, "What the fuck? Why don't you shut the fuck up?" And it'd be time for me to go to work. So, one day, it was time for me to go to work and he started cursing at me. So, he stood up over me. And I said, "Oh my God, he just don't know. He don't know me." He said, "I'm from Brooklyn." Because I lived up here a little while, he's going to make it seem like... I said, "I'm from Brooklyn, too. Don't put it like that." He said, "Blah, blah." I jumped up and he hit a nerve and I know I had to go to work. I'm not going to let it mess me up. I said, "You don't even work and you get almost $2200 a month, you know?" He made me so mad I jumped up and said, "Who the fuck you think you is? I gotta go to work." I said, "I'm from Brooklyn, too. I ain't scared of you. I ain't no punk bitch." He said, "Oh." I said, "That's right. Come on let's go. I ain't trying to be no man. But you're cursing me out like I'm a punk? I ain't no punk." I said, "You got the wrong kind of person. So, we get to [the shopping center where I work] right, all of sudden he said, "Well, we got no gas in the car." Well, I never had the car. I said, "What you say?" He said, "You can't put no gas in the car?" I said, "I don't drive the car." Please let's get to work. He jumps out and swings the car door. Now, I'm like, "You tearing my stuff up, too?" In my mind I'm thinking, "God forgive me please." I start singing and rocking and I get out of the car. He gets in the car and shoots off. When something happened to the car, he paid. I don't mind driving it, but he paid when something goes wrong with it. He'll take it to the shop. I said, "No problem. As long as I know you're going to pay for it." My kids are like, "You let him hold the car?" But he got money to pay for it. I know he got money coming in every month. Y'all, if something go wrong, you call me up, "The car is stuck. I can get on the bus." "Don't leave my car."

I had my kids staying at the house and the lights got cut off. Nobody want to pay the bill. Nobody want to clean up, so I ended up going over and cleaning the house out on Mother's Day, freezing and all. So, I moved the bed out, 'cause something wasn't right. He kept talking about, "We can both pay the bills," and stuff like that. He was helping to pay the insurance and out of nowhere he started getting high. When it was time to pick me up [from work], one day, I cried like a baby. It was snowing, I said, "Why did I do this Father? Why did I do this? Why did I let them bring me to work and it's snowing and everything and then leave?" I'm calling him and he's like, "I can't make it." What, it's only three blocks? I didn't want him to crash the car up. One of his friends brings the car back. He says, "I am so sorry, I told him." I said, "But, he still shouldn't have did that. That's wrong." I said ok. The second time I had to get the car out of the snow. I walked. My hands was frozen, my feet was frozen. I was so angry. And then I had to walk up to the third floor and knocked on the door. I said, "Give me my keys. Just give me my keys, please." I had extra keys. He gave me my keys. I got in the car. I cried. I rocked and I cried. I rocked and I cried. 'Cause my hands were so frozen.

But that wasn't it. After that happened, I had already moved home. I kept sending him to the VA hospital, 'cause he kept getting so high that I ain't trying to be there for no one who goes dying on me. It used to be like, "I don't know what's going on." I said, "Oh, no, no, no." He started doing all kinds of crazy stuff. So, I ended up taking him and signing him into the VA hospital. They asked him what kind of drugs he's taking. He said, "I was drinking." They said, "What kind of drug?" He said, "Crack cocaine and everything else." I'm like, "Jesus!" I ended up putting him in there. It happened three times. The third time when he goes, every time he goes, I start packing up clothes and taking them to my house. And this one particular time, I just got tired. I started every weekend, I'd go home.

I'd go home every weekend 'cause he lays in the bed all day. All day long... he'd sit in the bed all day and he wants me to cook. He wants me to fix breakfast and cook. I was doing that for a little while, but we were doing it together. He likes cooking and stuff like that and we worked together. But, then we stopped doing that 'cause he used his money more on getting high, and he would have me in the house asleep and he'd be out. He'd call me up on the phone and tell me he's coming through in a taxi and tell me this certain place and tell me to go give $100 so he could go back somewhere up here in Central Tower. They got everything up in there. You go to the store, the drugstore...they got everything up in those buildings. Every weekend he left. The last time they sent him way up North to this other hospital for rehabilitation. He gave me these papers to pick his checks up and put them in the bank. But what happened was, he had somebody with his credit card and they would use it to get the money out of the bank and use it to get high with. Then he going to tell me to go cash his check. And when I went to cash his check, he overdrawed it. I was responsible. They were like, "How you want to do this here." I'm like, "No. no, no, no. I don't want to cash this check." There was no place but there I could cash his check and show them the paperwork. But, they said he can't cash his check 'cause he owed this much on his account. The check was like for almost $900 and he overdrawed it for something like 800 something dollars. So, I told him. It was a clothing allowance. He got it every September plus the $2200. So, he was getting all this money. Where was it going? And his rent is only $300. Everything is included. Every single thing –internet, cable, light and gas. And it's a nice apartment.

He signed himself out. He stayed two weeks until the first of the month. At the first of the month, he be trying to get out of there. He comes back and slowly but surly, every weekend, every weekend. And then it stopped - I think around Easter or something like that. He had borrowed the car one day and I had came home. The clothes that I left there [at his apartment] were in the living room at my house. He took all my clothes and said, "You don't come over anyway. You don't do nothing. Here's your clothes." At first I felt kind of bad. But then I thought about it. You know how he really ended it. We both were driving the car and I was still doing my car payments…he was doing the insurance since he was driving the car. So, he made up an excuse that he had to take care of his son, 'cause his son just went to jail and he needed to go there. His other son was in college and his son was still getting money from the military.

From there, he stopped helping me out. He told me when we first met, he'd help me out with the bills and help me get to where I was trying to go to do things right. But every time we made up a plan to do something, like we used to go to the City to get clothing, name brand stuff, and he'd sell 'em. But, he wasn't making any type of money, because he'd give it to the military guys who are retired. And they didn't have no money 'till the 1st or the 16th and the other ones was the drug dealers. He'd give them free stuff. I got to a point, he was giving them his car. He got a truck and I was taking care of the car while he was in rehab. So, I'm gassing up two cars and taking it to work. But, he started giving it to the drug dealer to take it where he had to go. So, I came back one weekend, and he says to go to the police station because the guys he gave the truck to had a key to the house…and that's when I left. The drug people had the keys to the house, plus the truck. So, I said, "You know what? I'm not staying in this house while you got drug dealers. They might be coming to get you, 'cause you owe them money and you got me laying up in here, or in the shower and these people coming in!"

So, I left then and I didn't go back. I tried to explain to his sister. And I didn't speak to him for a good while after I left. He'd call up and say, "You don't think about nobody but yourself." I wasn't being selfish. I just got so tired. I wasn't trying to push the issue of making something go on that wasn't there. I said, "I don't love you, and you're not doing anything for me. I work every single day. I don't miss a day of work…You get your money every day and you get insurance from head to toe from Veteran's, so, go argue with them." So, after that, we separated from that. I had to get away from that. I said no, I always attract the wrong kind. If I don't attract drug dealers, I attract a dope fiend!

Sonia
Feeling These Feelings and Living This Way

Some of the things [that have happened to me] feel as strong as the day it happened as a child. There's a lot, as I look back, that I'd do different, as far as my kids... I wouldn't have gotten into or turned to the drugs. I would have went a different avenue. But some part of me, I feel like I'm still kind of stuck when I'm moving ahead. But, I'm still kind of stuck because of one particular, the identity thing. I let my fear of what happened and no family – I have family, but not accepted and not a part of. I see that a part of me didn't really, because of things missing, or feeling like, "Ain't nobody gonna be there to enjoy so, why?" I didn't get into things, or give it my all like I should. So, now I'm at the point where I'm like, "Do you want to go another 40 years feeling these feelings and living this way?" I'm like, "No." I've come to the decision where I'm like, I got to make peace. But making that peace is like, it's hard. I need to let it go and move on. But, at the same time I'm like, "Ok, how do you do that when you still need answers? You don't know who you are. You still gotta go down these avenues." So, I'm like OK. Maybe this is my cross I have to bear in life. Maybe I need to start looking at it in a different way, instead of negatively, like I have all these years. Maybe I gotta start looking at it like, I can't say I'm from here or from there. I can be anyone, I can be from anywhere. But, at the same time, I don't want to take on that thought and get crazy with it. Sometimes it's confusing. And at the same time, I'm still in the middle of it. I'm thinking I've let it go, but then it don't feel like I did. It feels like I'm in the same place, and I don't wanna be.

I called Sylvia Brown. I started reading her book and in the back of the book there's a number. In my mind I'm like, "If she's a real, true psychic, maybe she could give me some leads on something." Only to find out, 'cause of how big she is, you don't get to talk to her. I couldn't even afford Sylvia. So, I got an address and I'm going to write her a letter, but I'm not even sure she'll see the letter. I'm like OK, that's not gonna work out. I was really, really hoping maybe I can get with a psychic or someone who can talk to the dead and I can get some answers. I even thought about maybe I should do the hypnosis thing and get some answers...just looking at other avenues to take instead of being these past 40 years...I'm tired of being confused, and depressed and fearful. Then, I'm happy one minute and then....

It's very hard to see [my future without answers]. I would like to say, "Oh, I see myself doing this." But, honestly, it's really hard to picture, 'cause I always picture myself alone. I have this new affirmation I've been telling myself: "You're not a failure." There are so many things. I should be at a certain point at this age. So, I'm like OK, if I am on Social Security or Disability, I want to at least have a job, be working, doing something more positive instead of always like I am now. In my own home, possibly, or working towards it, not still on Green Street. In school, have my diploma, my high school diploma. [I think about] possibly starting a business - something to take care of myself. I'm looking at well, disability ain't always going to last. So, I have to do something. I want to be happy. I don't want to be depressed or confused five to ten years from now. I want to think on it, "That's how it is." But I'll be at peace with it. I don't want to be envious, just glad to be alive, helping others, or whatever my career is at that time and enjoying the rest of my life. But that seems very far.

Sonia
Life Without a Mother

I would have more confidence in myself. I want to believe that my mom would have taught [and] that would have been instilled in me. I had guidance but, it wasn't to bring out who I was. I'm not sure what words to kind of put it. Yeah, I had the guidance, but the guidance was, "You do what I say, how I say it." And If I had...when I saw other families, I could never question nothing and if I did, I was called names, wasn't ever sat down and explained things. Say, for instance, when I just wanted attention or just wanted to hear someone say, "I love you, I'm proud of you." Or even if I did something wrong, if they said, "This is why this was wrong, what you did. You shouldn't do it, because this will happen," I was yelled at, called names. "You ho, you slut, you just want to sit around grown folks." And I would be, "I just want to hear that you love me. I want attention." "Oh, no you don't."

So, I feel like if my mom was living, I feel like she wouldn't have turned me away. Things I got negatively, looked for in the streets and possibly the weed...I would have got it naturally. I would have got it unconditionally from her. I would have more confidence. I feel like I wouldn't be depressed. She would have taught me. I would have completed things. When I got into things, I would have stuck it out. I wouldn't have given up so easily.

I never felt safe. 'Cause your child is given to feel safe, that no one would hurt them. Even though I couldn't even tell you what that feels like. Wow. I guess that's why I fear everything. Cause' when you don't get that, that's a big piece that comes from a mother to a child... sense of security or safety. Even though he or she goes out to the world every day, leaving, they still know that they're safe. Even though they'd be scared and afraid, somehow, the parent instills through their encouragement, helps you to instill that courage and strength you need. But, because I didn't have that, I had to somehow learn it on my own. Now, I know I learned it the wrong ways, but negatively and it got me through. But, now, where I'm standing, I'm learning that no, that wasn't right, because when I've learned how to get things in a negative way, I missed out on so much. It took me down a different path that I never wanted to go down.

It's funny, because the parent was one of, he was...and it's funny, I don't even want to call him my parent, because I still don't know whether he was my dad. And he was the one who took me. But, he was also the one who was leaving me here and there and didn't even care what was going to happen to this child, this little girl. And half the time he didn't stay around long. He dropped me off and he left. And when he left, all hell broke loose. I mean, sometimes, it was nice when the females, I can recall one or two was nice. But the majority of the time, there was always men around and I was always looked at as a piece of meat.

I was always taken advantage of. I guess it got to the point, when I got older and got on my own, I continued. It's funny 'cause it just hit me, I just continued the same sick cycle, when I couldn't get a job. I kept at that point, using as an excuse, "I don't have a birth certificate, so I can't do this. So, I got to..." To me it felt right, selling my body. What it did to me on the inside, I would look past myself when I looked in the mirror. Couldn't stand myself 'cause of what I just did, couldn't stand the people - the men that I was laying with, but I knew I somehow had to take care of myself.

So when you're a child, what I have learned and seen, when that child doesn't get, and it's most important, I guess the rearing, from the parent...if my mom would have been here, I wouldn't have been a ho, a prostitute. I might have, who knows, smoked weed. I might have. I might have took a drink. But, I wouldn't have gotten into it so early in life, to where my personality and the character and educating and learning – I wouldn't have given up on it. Because even with school, now that I think about it, I just went. It was a place I could go where at least a few hours there wasn't nobody yellin' at me. Even though I went through stuff in school, it was peaceful. It was kind of like freedom. But, even though, at a certain time I had to go back. Every day it seemed like the closer I got back to being at the house, every day, I remember I used to wish there was some place else I can go. The weed - the using the drug helped me to cope and to deal with it.

Gloria
Becoming a working woman

It was...a summer job when I turned 15. It was for Father Powell's...a church that was in Brooklyn, New York. All the youth, kids were over there. And that was my first job. That was my first time getting a Social Security card. My sister-in-law, she was 14, she was my brother's wife and we all met when we had the youth job at apartment buildings, two apartment buildings where we lived at between St. John's and Sterling. What they got a group of kids that lived in the building, since we didn't go out to certain areas that you can get summer jobs and stuff. We got it over there in the building and we worked until like, what, the end of August and saved up money and everything to get school clothes and whatever we had to do. We socialized with the people who lived across from us. They lived in 505 Howard Avenue and I lived in 510 and then my father moved over into the next building. There was two buildings right next to a little grocery store. So, you come out of the building and right into the grocery store. Across the street, my girlfriends live in 505. That was a big building too.

Then, on the corner, there was so much going on on that corner. Back then, the thing was a big thing with people shootin' drugs. That corner was the main corner. From the roof down to the basement, everybody [was] in and out that building, back and forth, back and forth. There was so much going on out there. You would see so much shootin' and everything, and then you see everyone standing on the side just nodding back and forth. That went on a lot. But, we didn't pay them too [much] mind. They were on their side of the street. We were on our side of the street. When certain things happened like that, my father opened a thing down in the basement where we could play at. He made a stereo out of crate boxes and he made a little bar thing. We was too young to drink. He made a little stage...he was a carpenter. So, he made a little stage, with a little wall with a little light right there. There were two little tables down there. We used to go down there all the time and play and stuff. He was the Super, my father, and way in the back they had, like...an apartment down in the basement. The last room was like, yay high. We used to play hide and seek and crawl up under there like that...be ducked down. It was something we enjoyed for a long time.

After a few years, we ended up going to this other place that was up town from where I lived at. It was near the shopping area, Picking Avenue where they have this church, it was on Bristol Street. It was called Faith, Hope and Charity and they had another set of teenagers. I think I was 16 or 17 then. I went over there to work for them. I was in the crowd taking care of the younger kids... They'd take the kids on trips and stuff, just like they do out here.

I was about 18. I started hanging out with my girlfriends and stuff like that. I'd hang out all night long and try sleep all day. And that's what I'd do with my girlfriends. I used to go to a club around the corner called the Red Light, and then there's another club down the street called the Blue Light, and I used to hang in those clubs so much. And at that time, I didn't think about anything else. I was staying with my step-mom. I didn't stay with my mom, because my mom was living on the other side of town and she drank a lot. So, she wasn't able to raise me. So, I went to my step-mom and my father over there. I ended up pregnant, and I was going on 18 and that's when I had my first child. After I had her, my step-mom helped me raise her and stuff, and then, after a while, I knew I had to go back to school and get a job or do something.

So, what I did was, I started going to the training programs. I used to go to Adelphi Business School and all those. There were different ones, and I didn't stay with it. I stopped like any other teenager, because I didn't have someone right there to explain to me exactly, "You got to keep going and get yourself together. You got a child now. Do what you have to do." I didn't get that chance to hear that from nobody at that time. I had step-brothers and sisters and I stayed with them, and we all slept in the same room. When I got pregnant, I finally got my little room in the hallway.

I let my mom take care of my baby for a little while and I started running the street again, and hanging out with my girlfriends. Then, the baby's father, what he wanted to do is... his girlfriend wanted to raise my older daughter. So, what I did, I took her over there, 'cause what I wanted was to go out partying. So, they started raising her. After a while, she was so used to her she was calling her mommy. I didn't like that, but I accepted it, because I was going on my next chapter.

That's when I realized I had to get out of my mom's house, either get a job or do something. So, I ended up going on Social Service and I had my second child. At the time, I had my second child, I got on Social Service, I moved into an apartment building and everything. I was on Social Service for a while. All I did was stay in the house and watch the stories and I didn't think about anything else. I didn't know anything else at the time. No one said, "Well, why you doing this? You could be doing this, doing that." All the things I'm doing now, I should have been doing back then. But I didn't know it, because my mother came from the low of being on Social Service, too. At the time that you don't have to be on Social Service looking for somebody else... So, all the time all that stuff was going on, I ended up moving into an apartment building, four apartments on each floor. It was a big building. I lived in East New York and Ralph Avenue. This was in Brownsville. It was a nice area, but I lived smack dab in the middle of Brownsville. I had my son on the 21st and I brought him home on Christmas.

Once my son got to a certain age, he got to 2 or 3 years old. What happens was, my daughter comes all the time, she comes to visit. She'd have a little snappy attitude. I'd be doing her hair, and I'd be like, "What's going on? What's going on?" "I want to go home with my daddy." I'm like, "Something's not right." So, I have my aunt, "You better go get your daughter. They're going to think that's their baby." My aunt, she's a little agitated, and she's going on. I hung out with her mostly. So, finally, "I'm gonna go get my child." I went to go get my child and my aunt was there. I didn't do it the right way. They lived in the projects. So, I had to run through the elevators...she's screaming and hollering and I felt so bad.

She's screaming 'cause she don't want to be with me? I was like, "Wow." So, finally, they're saying I'm stealing their child. So, what I did was went to court. I did it the right way. I went to court and they told them they could have her on the weekends. But, I have to have my child back, 'cause that's my child. It doesn't matter. I did get her back and everything like that, and we made an agreement. I would come over there. She would come by and pick her up. It went like that for a long time until she got a certain age.

When she got to a certain age, I done had another child since then. But, the child died. I woke up one morning and the baby was blue. I was screaming and hollering cause the baby always wake up in the middle of the night, but it was daybreak outside and I'm like, "What is going on?" So, I'm rubbing the baby and I'm like, "Why the baby so hard and stiff? What the hell?" I though, oh. I called the ambulance and stuff and they're trying to blow in the baby's mouth, blow in the baby's mouth, and everything. So, they said, "Crib death." I said, "He wasn't in the crib!" Then I said, "You all called me a few weeks ago talking about you need to see me, 'cause his blood test." They said, "Well, he was anemic." But, nobody could tell this would've happened to me like that? I ended up pregnant the next year. He look just like him, just like the last one. He was born January the 6th and died April 4th. I had no money to bury him. So, they put him where the prisoners are buried. People on top of each other or something. I never got the death certificate. I never got nothing. I have to pay for it and I never got it. I said, "You all just took him. I didn't have a funeral. I didn't have anything. Nothing." His name was Christopher. He would be 37 years old.

After that, I had my son Sam. He was premature. I used to fight all the time with the father. Constantly. He used to stay out, stay out, stay out. Since he was one of those handsome, good looking guys, I didn't want to leave him. He was the kids' father and he would go out with his father number running. Back then in Brooklyn, they called it number running, because it was horse racing but it was illegal. It's just like anyplace illegal doing something like gambling not in the right place. But, that's how it was. He was like that. He used to like sleeping pills. He used to like something that always bring him down. Skin popping and stuff like that. With my kids, I don't have any type of, nothing be in the kids' system since I had the kids from him. But, after a while, he used to go to the Methadone program and stuff like that. He'd come back and get all mad and everything. And the little bit of money I get from Social Services, he'd want some of it. I can't do that. That's when I went through all the beatings and domestic stuff. I went through it a lot with him, but I'd always end up right back with him. Like one of them stories like, "Women like that." No, I didn't like that. I just didn't know what else to do, or who else to go to.

My mother used to tell me, "I go through that all the time." She said, "I don't understand it, but maybe because I drink." She said, "You have no reason to be going through that in your life, with no man. Before I leave this earth, you will leave that man. I'm not having you leave me before I leave here." And that's how my mother ended up dying.

It's going through my whole family, because my older daughter was going through it, too. But now, she's engaged to someone that's not like that. This person cooks for her, help her, rub her feet, everything. I'm like, "I wanna find a man like that." He's from the islands. He's really good. He's real nice – he likes to eat. She likes to eat, too. The both of them like to eat. My granddaughter likes to eat, so they're all trying to outdo each other eating.

My mother went through that. My younger daughter was going through that a few years ago. This one, Chantel, she's a stubborn one. She ain't letting anyone do nothing to her. Even though, she's got one hand, a severe right. Let 'em try it. Chantel's a strong one.

She got shot back in 1993, September of 1993. Seven years old. And I said God got a purpose for her, 'cause after that happened with her. [It happened] at a Chinese restaurant. I just moved up here. I just got my job working as a CNA ... it was in the newspaper here, too. I had to travel from here. I had to leave every weekend and drive up there to the ICU. They used to complain about me being in the bed with her. She had a bandage around her head and it was itching really, really bad. She'd be wet and everything. They had the old type of hospital. The office is around the corner. She was the only child up there on that floor. When I got there and saw all this was happening, I rang the bell and sat there. I done changed her and everything. I was going to school for CNA. I already knew, you put the bed pan there. All I needed was clean bandages and they told me "You can't touch it. It'll get infected. She's running a fever." But, I'm like, "How would you know? She's ringing the bell and you're cutting the light off me."

She was only a seven year old child. All that [the gunshot to the head] affected the one side of her body. It hit the front part... and came out on the side. It went through. I don't know how she survived all that, but God was with her. So when it hit that... her face all that one side, her arm. This one arm, she don't use it, and the Doctor told her, "If you don't use it, you'll lose it."

She was at Sunnyview. Every hospital from up here was calling down there trying to get her to put her in there. She was only going to the hospital to get her voice there and to get her walking back. She was home in November for Thanksgiving [having been shot in September]. They had her in the newsletter. I was taking her back over to Sunnyview to take her back for treatments and all that stuff. She had to go to special schools. I was like, what do you want me to do? I have to pay bills and stuff. I was living in Troy and they used to come pick her up in a car to take her to school, because she couldn't get on the bus with everybody else. She had to have to take pills for brain injury. When she'd have a seizure, her seizures were staring. She'd go into a stare and sit there. Seizures, they said, don't just be where you jump around and I said, "Serious?" With Chanel, it was a staring one. You'd think she's looking at you, but she's not there. After a while, she didn't need the medication. But, they said she have to have it. But, I said, "You giving her something that will set off something else." She's really, really strong minded... since she's a baby, three years old. She used to sit up in the middle of the night and ask,

"What's the matter? Why you not asleep? What's wrong? I'll help you. I'll rub your back."

She done put herself through school - got her associate degree. Right now, she's in [a hospital working], since her internship. She's still at the job she got through the internship, because she was really smart. But she felt, she wasn't getting the money...she likes nice stuff. She likes to work. She worked at [a grocery store], plus she worked at the other job. Nothing stops her. It could be snowing - she's still going to work. She bought herself ski pants and she still goes. It doesn't matter if she rides with me, or takes the bus. She don't care. "I don't need you for nothing," that's her words. She keeps going and she brings it back to me. She says, "Why you say that when you know you can do it?" I'm like, "Oh well."

Sonia
The Worst Advice I Ever Got

Every day, when I came home from school, I had homework. I would ask Martha (that was the man Robert's mother's mother) and I would have, like for instance English. I would ask for help, "You're the one in school. I ain't." And so, I was made, "Don't you move from that table until you're done." I would sit there and I would always have some music playing, 'cause for some reason, music would always just soothe me. And sometimes, I would feel a little smarter when I played music. And I sat and tried and figured it out on my own. And that's another thing, 'cause I just found out in doing that, I learned how to do things backwards. And when that child doesn't have that parent sitting there with the child…sitting there like, "No that's not right. This is how you do it."

When the child doesn't have that person to show them, they don't know if they're doing it right or wrong. But they'll keep on trying to do it. But at some point, that child will get tired of being alone, because when you're small everything is huge. It's like, to the tenth or twentieth power. And scary is not the word for it. Terrifying. So, any way to get rid of that terrifying feeling… he or she is going to do it somehow. It may not be right at that point and time, but to them it seems right. At least they're doing something. I knew I had to. I didn't want to give up, but I didn't have anyone, so I had to. And then there was I just wouldn't go. I wouldn't do it, 'cause I knew there wasn't no one at home who was going to help me. I had to do it on my own, and I didn't know what I was doing. So, it got to the point where I was going to school and class less and less.

Now, as I look back, it's very important for the parents to, even when it's hard or just one parent. Like my grandmother, or it's even harder when it's a grandparent, and they didn't get that much schooling. Then, it makes it even worse, because she's there and she may want to help. But, they may have limited schooling themselves, so the child is still on their own. But, when they got that parent, even though they may have limited schooling, they're still helping, [and] will push. As I look back now, even if I had that, I still would have been pushed in the right way. Maybe I would have stayed in school. I would have stayed after school more, or asked for help from the school. But even in schools, there wasn't, I guess, they don't pay attention. I think they don't pay attention to the student. If the student doesn't do the work, it comes out, but they're in school, in class. For me, it's not that I didn't want to do it, or skip class. It's just, for one, I didn't want nobody to know what I was going through. Kids can be very cruel, especially if the child was already being teased. So, the child's not gonna want some other kids to think, "Ok, I don't know this", 'cause then you're categorized as stupid, slow, you don't know this. So, I just stopped going, 'cause I didn't want to be put in the slow class like I was dumb or retarded or anything. A lot of times I just didn't go.

I can remember when I was first given to Robert's, mother's mother, when they started getting checks for me, I didn't have money. I would see the other kids getting stuff and I would want stuff. For some reason, I was always around grown folks, and I remember this one lady, I think she had a daughter and I was at her house. I can remember saying I don't have this and I need so and so. She gave me something to eat, or I might have been sitting down smoking weed at that time and she said to me, "Sweetie, I'm a tell you, I've learned you may be young, but you got to use what you got to get what you want. That way you won't have to worry about needing anything." And I was a child and it sound good, 'cause she was saying, "Oh you pretty. You got a nice body. You can use that to get what you want from it." And to me, I was like, "For real? I can get money?" But she failed to say the bad. Yeah, it was a quick way to get money, but then I'd be prostituting, selling myself, laying with men for money. I was eight.
After I did it, I got happy each time, because I had money. I didn't feel bad, or was teased 'cause of what I had on. But, then at the same time, even though I did it, I couldn't spend the money on anything new, because how was I going to explain where I got this money? So, I ended up spending the money on weed, drinking, candy, little stuff, or hiding it. When I left, when I went off to school in the morning, that's when I would spend it.

For a long time, I did that just to live, to have money in my pocket, to eat, for a hotel. Then when the drugs got in, and came into play, I did it for drugs and food. It was quick money, but I regret that. If I could see that lady today, I'd slap her. Like, how dare you? Don't you ever tell another young child, especially female, to use her body.

Sonia
The College Graduate

I went down, I made plans ahead of time to go down, bought the bus ticket like 3 months in advance. I took the Greyhound, which was supposed to been 22 hours. It ended up being 24 hours, which was cool. I like traveling and seeing different people, you know, meeting different people on the road. When I got there, the plans I made, the reservations at the Eco Lodge there in Conway, I ended up having to switch and get a hotel in Myrtle Beach... They told me when I called the day before that it was four miles either way from the Eco Lodge to Coastal Carolina, which was the university that my daughter was graduating from for music theater and arts, and dance. Come to find out, it was 15 miles and the taxi was starting off at $30, and depending on the traffic it was like $60.

So, the good thing is, I met this young lady named Crystal and another young man traveling from New York down to Myrtle Beach, South Carolina. The young man - it was his birthday and Crystal was going to see her relatives. She had a grandmother and some uncles there, which was cool, because by the time I got there I was really worried. All the plans I had made now, I had to make total different plans - meaning I had to switch hotels, was worried about transportation and which hotel I was going to be in. I didn't know, first time being in Myrtle Beach. It was a blessing that I met Crystal, because it was like she has an uncle, she got family, so it ended up that she was like, "Don't worry about it. We'll get you in a nice, cheap hotel and we'll get you set up, and you don't have to worry about anything."

So, her uncle picked us up from the bus station, which was shocking to me, because being up here in New York, people are so mean. It's like, he just welcomed me and so, it's like I'm a part of the family, 'cause I was with his niece, Crystal. So we went out to his house, had a couple of cocktails before I checked into the hotel. The uncle brought my bags into the hotel and helped me out then we went out to his house, had a couple of cocktails. Crystal and her uncle went by the grandmother's house. I met the grandmother and the hospitality is so great down there. They was eating some of the coffee cake with icing on it and they were like, "You want some?" And I was like, "No, no, I'm not hungry," which made me feel so good, 'cause I hadn't had treatment like that in years. So, me and Crystal, we went back to my hotel and put on our bathing suits and went down to the beach. And it was so fun, 'cause even being with Crystal, it felt like I had a sister. For once, they didn't know me and just welcomed me, as though I was a part of their family.

Then, the next day was my daughter's graduation. I was happy and worried at the same time, not knowing how [my daughter's] foster mom was going to act, or worried about what was she going to say. And the at the same time, I promised myself, no matter what, I was going to be happy… wasn't going to go off and get angry 'cause I know I got a temper and my mouth can have not good things come out of it. So, I'm glad I did pray, because the graduation was at the college on the football field. As we going to the bleachers, they're marching in and it was hot. The sun was drop kicking you, upper cutting you, body slamming you, and there was no shade. But I'm like, "I don't care, my baby graduating." So, we were sitting in the bleachers. Before we got to the bleachers, we was walking by where the football players get on the field and that's where the graduates were coming in though. I was going to stop there and try to get a picture of my daughter as she's marching in. That's when the foster mom came out with, "Don't push it. Don't push it. You're going to push her away." And I wanted to go off. But, I'm like, "No. Ok, yes, Ma'am." There were people around us and I was feeling very embarrassed. Because she wasn't – Southern people tend to be loud. So, we went on and sat down in the bleachers. The sun was just slapping the sh** out of us, oh, the "it" out of us. So, we're sitting there, and it's like four of us: The foster mom, and adult kids now, who have their own kids. And for some reason, the foster mom wanted me to sit next to her and I'm like, "Why?" and they're like, "I don't know." I didn't make no fuss or nothing. I sat down next to her. But, we was like sardines. When I sat down, she got closer. I'm like sitting there fanning and hinting, "You know, we're like sardines, here," hoping somebody'd move over, and nobody moved over.

And every time it seemed like she moved closer. And I had to say, "Excuse me would you move over, please? There's a lot of space." And she did. We're sitting there...and you know my big mouth. I'm my baby's cheering squad. I'm hollering.

Near the end, a Senator, a black Senator spoke and when he congratulated the mothers about how good they did with their kids, I felt kinda bad then, 'cause I hadn't really been around for 12 years. So, I was like, "Do I really have the right to stand up?" Even though I gave birth to her... I was tussling with that. And when he said stand up, a little voice said, "No, you stand up. This is still your baby." But, then the foster mom turned her head and gave me this monkey look. I looked at her out of the corner of my eye and I screamed by baby's name even louder.

So, everything's done. They finished the speeches and the graduates are marching out. So, we leave the bleachers to go down there and meet my daughter. So, as we're standing and standing and I'm trying to wait patiently, but anxious at the same time, and smiling like the Cheeto cat. Me and the foster mom are standing side by side. I had brought some yellow roses to give to her, 'cause I didn't have a gift. So, I'm waiting, me and foster mom side by side, and as [my daughter's] walking over to us, the foster mom with all these people standing around, she deliberately pushed me and grabbed and hugged her. And I'm like, "Really?" I just looked up at the sky. I didn't go off. I held my peace and [my daughter] walked over to me. And I gave her her roses and told her I loved her, and we put our arms around each other. It felt oh, God, I thank God. I'm still in awe. It feel so good is not the right word to use. It was so happy to feel my baby's arms give me a hug. I didn't know how the reaction was going to be – whether I was going to be the outsider or, you know...

But, I'm glad 'cause I really was welcomed in, except for I knew the foster mom didn't really want me there. She acted like she was nice and cordial and tried to get information out of me this time. But, I was like, "Nope." I learned from the first time that I shared a little bit too much with her. So, this time when she got to questioning, I was like, "Oh, everything's ok."

And I didn't give her no information, which was good. At the same time, for once, I didn't do what I would normally do, which was go off and flip out. I actually was quiet and I got to see God working.

After the graduation, I went back to the hotel. They dropped me off and [my daughter] was having a cook out at her apartment. So, I had a couple hours and Chrystal came by and we went to the beach again. Had a couple of cocktails at the beach at the bar, which was fabulous.

[Then I] came from the beach and I got dressed, and they came to pick me up for [my daughter's] for the cookout, all her sisters and foster sisters and brothers and foster mom. Her foster mom also had a catering business, which is great, from being all those years raising kids, she was able to build her own business, which was fabulous.

Near the end of it, which was a good thing, that all the foster sisters and brothers gathered around in a circle and said something positive over her life for her future. But, one thing I didn't like. When it got to the foster mom, she spoke last. When it got to her, one of the girls, one of [my daughter's] foster sisters, she had just graduated from college the year before, and now she's a big boss in this big plant down south. But, what I didn't like that the foster mom said was, she told [my daughter] she was proud of her, she was doing a good thing, she never gave her no problems, she was a good child. And I'm like shaking my head saying, "Yeah." And then, she said she used [the foster sister] and said "You should be like [the foster sister], because you know you never know when you're graduating. She couldn't find a job and now she's a big boss. You should get with her." To me, growing up, I always had people pointing and saying, "You should be like this one, or be like that person." Through my life, I've always tried to be like this one, be like that one, try to fit in there. And I didn't like that, 'cause I didn't want that for my daughter. I wanted her to be – I felt that was wrong, 'cause everybody don't have the same not-so-good luck. Just because it was hard for [the foster sister] to get a job, that don't mean it's going to be the same for [my daughter]. So,

I didn't say nothing, kept my mouth shut. Everybody gave each other hugs and left.

The next day, which was Sunday, Mother's Day, the whole time I'm thinking that my bus leaves Sunday evening at 6:30. I never checked the ticket, but I just know I'm leaving at 6:30. So, I got up and Chrystal's grandmother picked me up for church that morning.

After the graduation, Chrystal asked her grandmother can she give me a mother hug, because after I was in the hotel, and I didn't let them see me. No emotions or anything... I just let it all out when I got back to the hotel. When her grandmother hugged me, it was like my own grandmother was hugging me. She was like, "It's going to be alright." I hadn't even talked to the woman, "Just keep doing what you're doing. It's going to be alright." So, when she picked me up Sunday, it was a little church there in Myrtle Beach. You know how you first walk into church, she didn't sit down in the congregation in a little wooden chair. She went straight to the pulpit and I'm like, "Look at God." That's when I realized she was a pastor. God had placed a pastor in my path on this trip. That's when I realized God spoke to me through the pastor. And I know that was God. The whole time I walked in the church I was in tears. Then, when the pastor prayed and laid hands on me, that was it.

Backing up and getting back to the cookout, I realized when I kept quiet when my baby came over, "Mom, you ok? Mom, you ok?" I said, "Yeah, baby I'm alright." She asked me at the cookout ... did I want to see her apartment 'cause I'd never seen it. I said, "Yeah, you know I do." So, as we're walking she kept asking me, "Mom, are you ok? Mom, are you ok?" I said, "Baby, why you keep asking me that?" To my knowledge, I didn't know that she had [seen] everything that happened at the graduation. Actually, she thanked me for how I handled it. She said, "Momma, I want to thank you. I love the way you handled that, you handled that very well with class." And I said, "Thank you, Baby." I said to her, "You know I was determined not to let nothing ruin that day, 'cause it wasn't about me, nor the foster mom. It was about [you]." I let her know I personally thanked the foster mom. And [my daughter] said, "I didn't know that." I said, "Yes, I did." I told her I didn't mean no disrespect for the foster mom. I know she was there for 12 years, and I know she feel like this time is her time. But it's not. It's her day. So, any who, she asked me, "Did she say anything?" I told her what she had said, 'cause I didn't really want to. And she said [with a stern voice], "What did she say?" And I'm like "Oh, she is my child!" That's when I told her and she said, "Oh, did she?"

We went on. She showed me her apartment. She got the closets I would love to have. She got the walk-in closets. She got great taste. The apartment's got the water fountain, a fish pond, the private bath...oh, it's gorgeous.

Then, Sunday, Mother's Day, she called me and said, "Mom, I want to come," and her honey, my future son-in-law, which I thank God, he blessed her with a real man. A good man. He treats her like a queen. He opens the doors for her, close the doors for her. So, she took me out to dinner on Mother's Day to her job. Sitting there talking with her was....ahhh. It was the feeling like we had been in each other's lives. I'm older now. I get nervous when I talk to her, like, "What do I say?" I don't want to sound like an idiot, or crazy. But, I love the conversation that we had. I also got to let her know, she's making history. 'Cause she's from my genes, my lineage, and as far as my so-called dad, no one on that side, he didn't even make it past the 9th grade. As far as my mom, I'm still learning information about her, so to my knowledge, she's the first to graduate from college. And her older sister she's graduated, but she's making history. But, I had to let her know that, 'cause she didn't know that, but she does now.

That was our first Mother's Day dinner. We ate and then afterwards, when we left her job – she works at the Land Shark in Myrtle Beach, which is nice, right there by the beach, by the ocean, which is gorgeous. As we're leaving going back to the car, oh, my baby, she got a 2013 Wrangler. I'm like, "You go ahead." I felt so good 'cause my baby was driving me, it was Mother's Day in a brand new car she had just got. I wanted to stop to buy, 'cause I hadn't bought nothing as a souvenir. So she said, "You want to go in this store?" I said, "Yeah, 'cause I need to take a souvenir back, 'cause I haven't gotten anything." So, we went in and I look at a dress...so she said, "You see anything you like?" So, I walked to the back of the store and I started seeing the dresses with the wild animal prints, which I love. So, I picked out this hot pink dress. It's one of those stores where they're put a print on the dress for you. So, [the cashier's] like, "Ooh, I got one that's real nice for you." After she printed out the picture on the dress and I pulled out my money to pay for it, and was shocked and brought tears to my eyes, [my daughter] said, "Oh no, no, no. Put that back." I'm like, "Huh?" She said, "No, no. This is from me." I was like I just had to hold and kiss my baby. It's like the first Mother's Day gift I ever got. And I thank God.

That's my miracle baby. She's still doing great things. She's got a movie coming out. She's with MGM Studios and she has an agent. It's a beginning. It's a new beginning for me and her. I realize I gotta stay on my P's and Q's, meaning have the right people, do the right things, 'cause one thing I did realize is she's a no-nonsense young lady. And I love that about her. She's well-spoken. I love the way she carries herself. She carries herself, I like to say, just like a queen. She did such a fabulous job. I'm looking forward to a future together.

Gloria

Uncertainty

I'm in retail in a [shipping store]. We do a lot of printing and shipping, doing gallery pictures. I enjoy the job that I do and it's very nice and comfortable. But, what I do also is forwarding mail for our customers. We have all kinds of customers. International and inside regular areas like where I live at.

I've been at this job for nine years watching people leave, come, go, leave. I have learned by watching them the things that we do at the job. And my job was to forward the mail and answer the phones and do customer service and do other things in the store. But, the things they taught everyone else in the store was different. They did the print jobs and other stuff. They got paid more as they came in at that time.

We don't have benefits through the store because it's a franchise. Most franchises, it's up to them to decide to give you benefits and most of them don't, especially if you don't make a full 80 hours, even though you can get benefits over 35 hours or 32 hours or something like that. But, the franchise I'm in, we don't get paid for holidays or sick time or vacation. We don't get none of that. We still don't. The only time I got to go on vacation was when income tax time came. When I fill out my income tax, I save that money to go on vacation.

[Not having benefits and full time hours] caused a lot of problems, because a lot of my bills, and stuff like that, I barely made it. And with a lot of things I had to do, I used to have to get half of the money through a money order and then the next pay period I get the other half. But, still, I have other bills to catch up with. Then, it causes me to get something not being paid. Or, you know, something gets shut off. Half the time... if my lights don't get shut off, or [I get] an eviction notice to be kicked out, [there's] something else with not having enough food, trying to get medicine, trying to get food stamps and stuff like that.

With [an additional] part time job, it was overwhelming for me. What happened was from the timing, I was getting up in the morning, going to one job and needing to go to the next job, it was putting a lot of strain on me and my heart. I ended up with my blood pressure [rising] up and I ended up getting sick and then I had to stop with the job.

At this time, if I get another job, it's more strain on me with my blood pressure and hypertension and I get anxiety attacks. Getting a full time job, it's really hard to find someone that will be able to set me up at my age, for one thing. Plus, me being sick all the time, and then out, it's hard to...I could maybe get one, but I may not be able to persist on keeping that job from being sick. But, I'm praying I may be able to do that in the coming years and maybe months. I'm trying to look for something like that and at least retire in maybe five years, because I'm older now. I felt that the job that I have now should have been able to have some type of retirement or some kind of [401k] or something in behind there to look for when I retire, or leave the job.

I don't want to [move in with my daughter and her infant son], but right now, from me going through a lot, being sick, and not keeping up with my rent, and I'm not getting paid enough to keep up with the bills and stuff like that. We talked about it and decided that we have to find a two-family house with separate apartments or something like that. Or, find a house with four bedrooms with upstairs, downstairs or something like that. She makes a certain amount and I make a certain amount and we'd put our money together to try to do this here.

I'm really, really thinking about this, 'cause I'm tired of going through my things to catch up with my bills. With the lights getting shut down and then I have to repay and add an extra charges on that, and I'm trying to keep up with that. And then my rent - the same thing. I went through the time of going through an eviction because of something they made a mistake with. Then, now what's happening is, the changing ownerships at the job messed up my pay again. What happened is, I got paid for one week of pay for this week and my rent is due tomorrow, and I don't get paid again 'till next week. And now, I end up with another eviction notice. I can't win for either way. It's really crazy. So, that's why I'm thinking about either getting another part-time job, plus me and my daughter is looking for a house. I don't think it's going to work like that [living with my daughter peacefully]. Just the three of us...

Afterward
By Sonia Graham

I wanted my story told because, one, I wanted the world to know my story, because I felt like I was the only one who knew. I wanted to find someone who knew what happened to my mother, Rhoda Morgan and grandma, Ardie C. I want my mother to have a voice. Not knowing who I am, but who other people say I am, but not having the proof on paper, I want to know what other people know – their roots. I've always wondered "who am I?" I've always wondered, "Do I act like her. Do I look like her? What type of woman as she?" A crime happened when I was kidnapped. No one cared. There was no investigation – like she didn't exist. I know I exist, I know I'm here. But because there's no proof, I hope and pray that there is someone who has the proof. I refuse to accept that there is no answer.

Even though life is tragic and I can't live like normal people, life does go on. I may not be as happy as I'd like to be, I thank God I didn't give up. I just have to keep pushing on. If there wasn't a God I wouldn't be here to say this. Even through the tragedy, a lot of good has happened. I'm learning to accept through the crazy, accept life for what it is and still be kind. I'm more compassionate to other people, because of what I went through. My heart goes out to those who don't have mothers or families, who have been adopted. I know how it feels to be told that you're not wanted and not worthy. I grew up believing that. I grew up hating people. I want to tell people in my situation: "Don't give up. There is a light. There is hope." I've been taught through knowing people how to take that as strength and push forward. I want to tell people that what they went through is not because they're weak, but we have to watch our decisions. I realize that because of my choices it led my down roads I didn't want to go down.

But now, I thank God to see the beauty. I do feel hopeful for the future. I dreaded life. But I don't anymore. I felt like I wasn't like other humans, but now that I've heard other stories I don't feel alone. God has placed people in my life to teach me.

If there are answers or suggestions that could come from the telling of my story, which can lead me to know what happened, I would be open to hearing them. Please contact the author at larahammes@gmail.com if you know of my history or have an idea of how I can discover the answers to my kidnapping and identity.

Acknowledgments

First, and foremost, I have to thank Sonia and Gloria (whose name was changed for this book). They have told me their stories for many years, first in class, then on visits after they were students. Finally, through contact after I left the field, they eventually trusted me to record their interviews for what would become "Invisible Neighbors." They truly want people to know that life isn't easy for all Americans. I appreciate not only their time, but also their candor and bravery to tell of their struggles so that others may know.

Next, I have to thank my family for being behind me while I worked on this project. My daughter has been my biggest supporter, telling people, "My mom is an author." That's a big title to live up to. But, I hope that she will be proud when she's old enough to read this book. My husband has put up with me interviewing, writing and editing for what seems like an eternity. My parents and sister and mother-in law immediately bought the Kindle version, read it and talked with me about it.

Finally, I have to thank my friends. You know who you are. Those of you who listened to my stories and didn't roll you eyes, or tell me I was crazy and wasting my time. I have been privileged to have enough to be able to do this project. I hope, in some way, it can help those who don't have enough.

www.ingramcontent.com/pod-product-compliance
Lightning Source LLC
Chambersburg PA
CBHW070556290526
45790CB00002B/716